PREACHING NUTS & BOLTS:

Conquer Sermon Prep, Save Time, and Write Better Messages.

by Brandon Hilgemann

COPYRIGHT

Preaching Nuts & Bolts: Conquer Sermon Prep, Save Time, and Write Better Messages / by Brandon Hilgemann

Copyright © 2016 by Brandon Hilgemann, ProPreacher.com. All rights reserved.

For more information, go to ProPreacher.com

DEDICATION

To my beautiful wife, Taryn. You have supported me in ministry across the country and back, and put up with countless hours of my rants about ministry for over a decade. You are an amazing mother, and a greater wife than I could have ever asked for. I love you.

CONTENTS

Introduction	5
The Life of a Preacher	7
The Holy Spirit's Role	21
Know Your Audience	25
Be Yourself	34
The 7 Step Sermon Prep Method	41
Step 1 – Pray	44
Step 2 – Study	50
Step 3 – Focus	61
Step 4 – Illustrate	69
Step 5 – Outline	81
Step 6 – Edit	90
Step 7 – Practice	97
How to Get Ahead on Sermon Prep	106
Creating an Illustration Database	118
Conclusion	131
Learn More	134
About The Author	135

INTRODUCTION

When I first felt called to ministry, I had no idea what I was getting myself into. I had never preached a sermon in my life. I never had a mentor walk me through the process. In fact, I was scared to death of public speaking.

So I argued with God. I begged Him to let me do anything but preach. The thought of having to preach in front of a crowd every single week terrified me. But God didn't relent.

I went to a Bible college. I thought, "Surely, Bible college will teach me how to preach!" I applied myself. I graduated with honors with a ministry degree. But sadly, I was only forced to preach two times in the entire four years I was there. Since I was scared, I didn't go out of my way to seek preaching opportunities like I should have.

Suddenly, I found myself in my first job as a youth pastor. I immediately had to preach at least once a week. PANIC!

Bible college did not prepare me for this. What should I do? My first attempts at sermons (if you could even call it that) were horrendous. I stood in front of my notes, shaking while reading the message word for word.

This is not what I got into ministry to do! I needed to get better.

So I hit the books. I read every book on preaching I could get my hands on. The books were alright but mostly theoretical. So I asked a lot of pastors a lot of questions and started listening to as many good preachers as I could find. Finally, I started getting some practical advice.

Slowly, I began to get better with each message.

This little book is the kind of resource I wish I had way back when I felt the call to ministry. There were good books on preaching, but most lacked the practical tips I needed. I knew why I preached and what to preach. What I didn't know was how to preach.

I needed short, practical tips to get me started in the right direction.

Writing a sermon is not as complicated as it may seem. My hope is that this book will save you from the same panic attacks I had.

However, if you are a well-seasoned preacher, don't think this book isn't for you. It never hurts to get back to the basics. Writing this book has been just as helpful for me, reminding me of areas I, myself, have strayed from.

Thanks for taking the time to read this book. I cannot help but think your preaching will be better for it.

THE LIFE OF A PREACHER

> *"What is preaching? Logic on fire! ... Preaching is theology coming through a man who is on fire."*
> —Martyn Lloyd-Jones[1]

Preaching is so much more than eloquent words and a crafted presentation.

Preaching encompasses your entire life.

It cannot be just what you do. It is part of who you are.

You are not just a person who delivers sermons; you are a preacher.

There is a big difference.

---

[1] D. Martyn Lloyd-Jones, *Preaching and Preachers* (Grand Rapids: Zondervan, 2011), 110.

Don't misunderstand. The preparation and delivery of a message is important. But even more important is the life of the messenger.

"A prepared messenger is more important than a prepared message."
—Robert Munger

Only 1/3 of Preaching Is the Words You Say

Do you ever obsess over the words of a sermon?

If you are like me, you can sometimes spend hours trying to craft the best possible way to explain a Biblical principle.

We work like wordsmiths, trying to pound out the very best phrases.

But sometimes this can be a problem. Our obsession with words can cause us to lost focus on the other less obvious elements of a sermon.

Did you know that only 1/3 of preaching has anything to do with the actual words that come out of your mouth?

Blasphemy? Nope. Biblical.

The Three Part of Persuasion

First, we need to start with a brief understanding of Rhetoric, the study of persuasive speaking. All preaching is persuasive speaking. We are trying to change a person's thoughts or actions.

Good preaching is persuasive preaching. If not, it is just fluffy words with no power.

The Greek philosopher, Aristotle, taught that all persuasive speaking has three parts: ethos, pathos, and logos.

Put simply, these words can be defined as follows:

- **Ethos** = Character

- **Pathos** = Passion

- **Logos** = Words

Every person in an audience subconsciously evaluates the speaker by these areas to determine whether or not they will believe what the person is saying.

Evaluating ethos, the audience asks, "How do you live?"

Before a word comes out of your mouth, the audience needs to know that you are credible – a person of good character.

Why should they listen to you? Are you trustworthy? Are you respectable? What authority do you have to speak on this issue? Do your beliefs and actions align outside of church?

Evaluating pathos, the audience asks, "How do you feel?"

You can speak the most well-crafted words, but if the audience doesn't feel your emotional connection—your passion—it will fall on deaf ears.

Are you passionate about your message? Can the audience feel your passion? Does your message resonate with your audience on an emotional level? Has the message personally impacted you?

Evaluating logos, the audience asks, "How do you say it?"

Although logos is typically where most preachers start, the ethos and pathos are evaluated long before the audience decides to listen to what you even have to say. However, your words are still incredibly important.

Is the message clear? Does it make sense? Is there a logical flow? Are you speaking your audience's language? Is the message helpful? Is it applicable to your audience's daily life?

Ethos, Pathos, and Logos in the Bible

Right now, you may object to Aristotle's teaching. You may be thinking, "So what? Who cares what some Greek philosopher says?"

If so, you might be surprised to find that the Bible echoes this teaching.

Paul references all three parts of persuasion in 1 Thessalonians 1:5. See if you can find all three:

"our gospel came to you not only in word, but also in power and in the Holy Spirit and with full conviction. You know what kind of men we proved to be among you for your sake." (1 Thessalonians 1:5, ESV)

Paul says that he preached the Gospel not only in word (logos), but with full conviction (pathos), and proven character (ethos).

Paul understood that Gospel preaching is more than the words we say. A sermon is the sum of a preacher's character, passion, and words.

It makes sense, doesn't it?

Nobody wants to listen to a preacher who doesn't practice what they preach (ethos). We don't want to hear a sermon on marriage from a man who cheats on his wife.

Nobody wants to listen to a preacher who doesn't feel what they are saying (pathos). We don't want to hear a monotone sermon about living passionately for Christ.

Nobody wants to listen to a preacher who fumbles with words (logos). We don't want to hear a sermon that we cannot understand or is too random to follow.

So before you work on shaping your next message, does God first need to shape you, the messenger?

Is any area of your life lacking in character? Are you burning with passion for Jesus?

Only 1/3 of preaching is the words you say. 2/3 is the person you are.

Practice What You Preach

"Who you are speaks so loudly I can't hear what you're saying."
—Ralph Waldo Emerson

The longer I am in ministry, the more I see it. Another pastor has a moral failure that scars the church and murders his ministry.

Whether it's an affair, drugs, porn, or mishandling money, these hidden sins are ripping churches apart and leaving good people feeling betrayed and disillusioned.

Before we get into the practical tips on how to preach, we have to start here.

Integrity. Character. Self-control. Discipline.

Before you practice preaching, you had better practice what you preach.

The phrase, "Practice what you preach." is not a modern idea. It is grounded in Jesus' rebuke of the hypocritical Pharisees.

"For they preach, but do not practice." (Matthew 23:3, ESV)

My prayer is that nobody could ever say that about our ministries.

The stakes have never been higher.

Long ago, the title of pastor was respected. Today, the title of pastor no longer carries respect in the eyes of most people outside the church. It carries skepticism.

Trust has never been harder for pastors to earn. There have been too many fallen pastors that have ruined it for the rest of us.

This is not something to be taken lightly!

The Standard for Pastoral Living

"Not many of you should become teachers, my brothers, for you know that we who teach will be judged with greater strictness."
(James 3:1, ESV)

Becoming a pastor doesn't mean that sin no longer affects you. God doesn't suddenly grant you super powers to never have to face temptation again.

In fact, the Devil will do absolutely everything in his power to trip you up more than ever.

If angels rejoice every time a new believer is added to the kingdom of Heaven, you better believe there is a party in Hell at the fall of every pastor.

This is no joke. This is war!

A pastor must do their absolute best to follow all the commands in Scripture.

So what should the standard for a pastor's life be?

A great place to start is 1 Timothy 3:1-7.

Paul lays out the standards for being an "overseer" or elder in the church. These rules not only apply to elders as we see them in churches today, but all those in church leadership.

"The saying is trustworthy: If anyone aspires to the office of overseer, he desires a noble task. Therefore an overseer must be above reproach, the husband of one wife, sober-minded, self-controlled, respectable, hospitable, able to teach, not a drunkard, not violent but gentle, not quarrelsome, not a lover of money. He must manage his own household well, with all dignity keeping his children submissive, for if someone does not know how to manage his own household, how will he care for God's church? He must not be a recent convert, or he may become puffed up with conceit and fall into the condemnation of the devil. Moreover, he must be well thought of by outsiders, so that he may not fall into disgrace, into a snare of the devil."
(1 Timothy 3:1-7, ESV)

If 1 Timothy 3:1-7 doesn't fully describe you, what in your life needs to change?

Who Are You Really?

A while back, I was wrestling with my identity as a preacher. Who am I? What life am I called to live? What convictions must I stand for?

There are a lot of external expectations and pressures for how a pastor should look, act, and live. Most people in your church have an opinion of who you should be. But who does the Bible say you should be?

In an attempt to define what it means to be a preacher, I wrote what I call "The Preacher's Manifesto." A manifesto is simply a written declaration of beliefs or values.

This is what I firmly believe. This is what I stand for. This is who I vow to be as a preacher of God's Word.

When I feel the pressure of everyone else' opinions, I go back to my manifesto to keep me grounded. When I am feeling down on myself because I don't measure up to other pastors, this lifts my head back up.

Use mine, or, even better, go through the process of writing your own.

The Preacher's Manifesto

I am a preacher.

I am a messenger of the most high God – an ambassador of the Lord Jesus Christ (2 Corinthians 5:20).

I am a herald of the greatest story ever told, and the best news ever received (1 Corinthians 15:1-4).

I am a sinner, saved by grace—not through my works, but through Christ's work in me (Ephesians 2:8-9).

I am equipped with everything I need for the calling God has for my life (Ephesians 2:10).

I will preach the Gospel without shame (Romans 1:16).

I will not settle for moralistic, therapeutic, feel-good, prosperity preaching (2 Timothy 4:2-3).

I will preach the truth, the whole truth, and nothing but the truth of God's Word (Titus 2:1).

I will use the Bible as the firm foundation for all my messages (2 Timothy 2:15).

I will read the Bible more than best-sellers (Psalm 1).

I will study academically, but speak plainly for all to understand (Acts 15:19).

I will work to please God, not man (Galatians 1:10).

I will seek to be faithful, not famous (1 Samuel 12:24).

I will glorify God, not myself (1 Corinthians 10:31).

I will build up God's kingdom and His Church, not my own (Matthew 6:33).

I will live with the highest integrity—a life above reproach—so the Church won't get another black eye (1 Timothy 3:1-7).

I will practice what I preach (Matthew 23:3).

I will boast in my weakness, not my strength (2 Corinthians 12:9).

I will live in Biblical community, not isolation (Hebrews 10:24-25).

I will know and love my neighbors, not just my church members (Leviticus 19:18).

I will live, eat, and drink with sinners—like Jesus did—because it is not the healthy who need a doctor but the sick (Matthew 9:11-13).

I will prioritize the needs of my wife, sacrificing myself for her, so that ministry doesn't become my mistress (Ephesians 5:25).

I will spend quality time with my children, so they will grow to love the church, not hating it for taking their daddy (Ephesians 6:4).

I will honor the Sabbath and rest, knowing God is in control (Exodus 31:12-13).

I will circle my preaching in prayer, giving my anxiety to God (Philippians 4:6-7).

I will listen before I speak (James 1:19).

I will become all things to all people so that I might win as many as possible (1 Corinthians 9:19-23).

I seek to serve, not to be served (Romans 12:3).

I will give before I receive, because I will reap what I sow (Galatians 6:7).

I will truly love people, not just pretend to love them (Romans 12:9-10).

I will preach with all I've got, holding nothing back (Jeremiah 20:9).

I will not back down, shut up, or shy away from speaking the truth (Acts 5:40-42).

I will preach hard truth with love (Ephesians 4:15).

I will hold firm to sound doctrine, no matter how unpopular it may be (Titus 1:9).

I will not waver in my faith in a big God who accomplishes big things through those who dare to act upon God-sized dreams (Ephesians 3:20).

I will not allow temptation and the Devil to gain a hold on me (James 4:7).

I will be a living sacrifice (Romans 12:1).

I will fight the good fight, keep the faith, and finish the race (2 Timothy 4:7).

I am a preacher.

And, Lord willing, in the end, I will hear those words I so desperately long to hear: "Well done good and faithful servant" (Matthew 25:21).

What Do You Stand For?

Determine right now who you will be, what you will stand for, and how you will live out your calling as a preacher of God's word. Then, hold uncompromising to this Holy standard.

How you live each day will ultimately determine the effectiveness of your ministry and the legacy you leave behind.

THE HOLY SPIRIT'S ROLE

I once attended a new church with a friend. The people were friendly. The worship was good. But then I saw something I had never seen before.

While the band played, a man sat in the front row, scribbling feverishly on a napkin. When the music ended, the man stood up and walked to the pulpit.

The pastor then preached from his napkin!

He wrote his entire message during worship! I couldn't believe it.

To be fair, he was pretty good. He preached a decent sermon. However, I had never seen such a spontaneous approach to preaching.

When I asked my friend about it, I learned that this wasn't just a one-time thing. This is how the pastor prepared his message every week.

His reasoning for his unorthodox approach was that he let the Holy Spirit guide his messages. He preached as the Spirit led.

At first, this seems like a good answer. After all, it sounds very spiritual. But is that the best way to prepare to stand before your congregation and deliver the Word of God?

Is the Holy Spirit's power to speak limited to the worship service, or can He also speak a week, a month, or even a year ahead of time?

Proverbs 21:31 says, "The horse is made ready for the day of battle, but victory rests with the Lord" (NIV).

You cannot win without God. God brings the victory, but the horse must still be prepared for battle.

Soldiers who trust in the Lord for victory still train, strategize, sharpen their swords, put on their armor, and fight with everything they have.

Preaching is no different. We plan. We prepare. We practice. (We work hard to find words that all begin with the same letter.) Then we preach with everything we've got. And we are reliant upon the Holy Spirit every step of the way.

Preaching is 50% physical and 50% spiritual. Good preaching requires an equal dose of preparation and dependence upon the Holy Spirit. We must find balance between both.

The pastor who wrote his sermon during worship was a good preacher, but how much better could he have been if he was seeking the direction of the Holy Spirit while he prepared his sermon all week, instead of just on Sunday morning?

While writing your sermon notes during worship may sound extreme, I have also seen many pastors go the opposite direction. They study so thoroughly that they don't need God's help. They do it on their own.

We have to remember that God brings the victory. We should have a complete dependence on Him for our messages, but we still need to do the hard work of preparation.

We cannot use the Holy Spirit as an excuse for laziness, but hard work will also never compensate for a lack of God's work.

I once heard a pastor say, "Work like it depends on you, but pray like it depends on God."

That is the balance we need to bring to preaching.

The question isn't, "Should I be dependent on the Holy Spirit or preparation?" The question is, "Am I seeking the Holy Spirit and honoring Him in my preparation?"

Each of us would probably admit that we lean too heavily towards one spectrum or the other.

We must prepare the horse for war, knowing the battle belongs to the Lord.

KNOW YOUR AUDIENCE

"Many a preacher misses the mark because, though he knows books, he does not know men."
—James Stalker

All preachers should know why they preach. It's the Gospel. It's Jesus taking the punishment we deserved for our sins so that we can be made righteous before God.

I'm assuming we all get this. If not, put this book down and pick up a Bible.

Most pastors understand why they preach, but many pastors fall into the trap of neglecting who they are preaching to.

The Bible tells us that when Jesus saw the crowds of people, he had compassion on them because they were helpless, like sheep without a shepherd (Matthew 9:36).

Jesus' compassion for people motivated his preaching.

I imagine that Jesus, being God in flesh, didn't just see a faceless crowd before him. He saw each individual. He knew everything about every single person in the crowd. He knew each of their deepest, darkest desires. He knew their hardest struggles and hidden fears.

Jesus didn't just see a mass of people; He saw individuals who deeply mattered to Him. Individuals who deeply mattered to God.

So when Jesus preached things like loving your neighbor, not committing adultery in your heart, and not worrying about tomorrow, I believe He looked directly into the heart, mind, and soul of each person in the crowd and knew that these were messages they needed to hear.

Jesus knew exactly who He was speaking to. Do you?

Who is the motivation for your message?

Knowing your audience is a large part of sermon preparation. You must know who you are preaching to before you write a single word of your sermon.

If you are preaching this week on marriage, who are you preaching to? Is it Jeff who just had a messy divorce? Is it the clueless newlywed couple you did premarital counseling for that thinks marriage will solve all their problems? Is it Tanya, the single woman who is wondering if she will be single forever or if the next man who comes into her life will finally be "the one?"

If you are preaching on faith in suffering, who are you preaching to? Is it the Edwards family who just lost a child? Is it Esther, the elderly woman who lost her husband? Is it John, the unemployed father who cannot seem to find a job and is feeling hopeless?

If you are a youth pastor, who are you preaching to? Is it Austin, the middle school boy struggling with suicidal thoughts? Is it Jessica, the high school girl who is dealing with shame and grief after going too far with her ex-boyfriend? Is it Drew, the guy who pretends he is a sold-out Christian on Sunday, but parties hard Monday through Saturday?

Like Jesus, you need to know your audience. It is not enough to just know generalities and statistics. Who are you speaking to?

Get Out From Behind Your Desk

One of the most common mistakes that pastors make in sermon preparation is spending too much time behind a desk.

Yes, you need time for study, writing, and balancing the many other demands of ministry. But if you never get away from your desk, you will soon lose touch with your people.

You cannot get to know your audience from behind a desk. Sure Facebook, text messages, emails and phone calls are helpful tools. But they will never be able to replace real, face-to-face relationships.

Too many pastors know a lot about dead authors, but little about their audience. If they aren't careful, their preaching soon becomes irrelevant to the people they are called to reach.

This is the delicate balance of pastoral ministry. Too much time away from the desk and your ministry will suffer. Too much time behind the desk and your preaching will suffer— not from lack of preparation, but lack of connection.

Honestly, this is something I struggle with. My natural tendency is to be an introvert. I love to read, write, and create things. If I'm not careful, I can begin to see people as a distraction from my work instead of the reason I work in the first place.

Good preachers must have their finger on the pulse of their people.

Imagine Jesus working in the church today. Can you picture him sitting behind a desk all day? No way!

Ministry was never meant to be a desk job. The work is important, but people are the priority. We must find balance.

5 Benefits of Spending Time With People

There are five benefits to spending time getting to know people.

1. Relevance

A pastor who is disconnected from his people will soon be disconnected in his sermon.

Being able to drop the name of their favorite show, name a specific problem they face at work, or speak about a specific family problem they struggle with is what makes people feel like you truly understand them. It makes your message relevant to their lives.

2. Evangelism

The longer you are in ministry, the less non-Christian friends you have. If you want to reach people for Jesus, you have to get out and meet them.

If you are always in your office or at church, all of your interaction will only be with church people. Before you know it, you will lose connection with non-Christians.

You will forget how they think. You will forget how they live. You won't know the best way to reach them because you aren't hanging out with them. Soon you will be just another out-dated pastor.

3. Reputation

People don't care how much you know until they know how much you care. If you never talk to people in the community other than church members, you will just be another pastor in the mind of the community.

However, if you spend time in the community and get to know people, you will soon create a whole new reputation as the pastor who cares. Even if people disagree with your faith, they will appreciate your friendship.

4. Illustrations

People are a wealth of sermon illustrations. Get to know them well enough and they will share unbelievable stories of suffering, success, failure, and spiritual transformation.

A pastor who shares personal stories of people (with permission) is far more interesting than one who recycles canned illustrations from a book or website.

You can tell a pastor who spends time with people by the stories he shares.

5. Empathy

We have compassion for people we know. It's easy to look at a picture of a person in a foreign country and feel sad for them. But moments later you will move on.

However, if you travel to that country, meet them face-to-face, learn their name, meet their family, and see their struggle first-hand, you will be wrecked for life. You will have to do something, because now it's personal.

This is the same with the people in your community. Knowing their family by name, seeing their struggles, and helping them through tough times creates a bond. Your heart will expand for your community. You will feel their pain and be a better preacher because of it.

How to Get Out More

If you are like me, getting out of the office doesn't happen naturally. You need to plan ahead and set a schedule to make it a habit.

- **Delegate**. Find others who can take some of the work off your plate. Delegation frees up time so you actually can step away from your desk.

- **Never eat alone**. Schedule coffee, breakfast, lunch, or dinner with key volunteers or families every week. You have to eat anyway; you might as well enjoy some company.

- **Practice hospitality**. Find excuses to invite people into your home. Invite people over for birthday parties, football games, or holidays. Get creative or just invite them to hang out and talk.

- **Meet your neighbors**. Find an excuse to talk to your neighbors. Bake them cookies just because. Play with you kids in the front yard instead of behind a wall in the backyard. Take a lot of walks in the neighborhood.

- **Join activities**. You don't have to create everything. Get involved in things people are already doing. Join a local gym, sports team, club, or business network. Volunteer to coach your kid's sports team, help in their school, or serve the community through an organization that isn't connected to your church.

- **Be a regular**. Spend a few office hours every week in the same public place at the same time. Pick your favorite coffee shop or restaurant – somewhere other people hang out too. Get work done, but don't be so wrapped up in it that you shut out the world around you. Get to know the names of the staff. Talk to people around you. Maybe even eavesdrop on a conversation or two.

I know this isn't easy for everyone. Don't be overwhelmed. Just pick one of these ideas, and do it this week.

Put a Face on Your Sermon

Next time you write a message, put a face on it. Pick a person. Write down their name. Imagine this person while you write your sermon. Imagine their situation while you apply the message. Imagine their face while you preach.

When you do this, people will respond, "Wow, I felt like you were speaking right to me!" And you will think, "That's because I was!"

If one person in your audience is dealing with something, they probably are not the only one.

When you preach to one, you impact everyone. When you to preach to everyone, you impact no one.

Do you know your audience? Do you spend time with them? Have you had deeper conversations than, "How was your week?"

You must know your audience.

Knowing your audience is hard work. It is not something that can be accomplished in a week. Regardless, you have to think of it as a significant part of your weekly sermon preparation.

Who are the people you are preaching to?

BE YOURSELF

> "Natural delivery now rules the day. The preachers most respected are those most able to sound like themselves when they are deeply interested in a subject."
> —Bryan Chapell[2]

Years ago I bought a pair of knock-off Oakley sunglasses while on a mission trip to Mexico. I thought they were pretty cool.

They looked almost like real Oakley sunglasses, but were only a fraction of the cost.

I wore those beauties every day for a month. I looked good!

But after a month, they fell apart. The frame snapped. The lenses popped out. My cheap sunglasses were no more.

---

[2] Bryan Chapell, *Christ-Centered Preaching: Redeeming the Expository Sermon* (Grand Rapids: Baker Academic, 1994), Kindle edition, location 7405.

So what did I do? Hoping for a different result, I bought another pair on my next trip to Mexico. But the same thing happened. A month later they fell apart.

Real Oakleys don't do that, but mine were a cheap imitation.

I tell you this cautionary tale, because I fear that too many pastors setlle for cheap imitation preaching.

Years ago, if you wanted to hear a well-known pastor preach, you had to travel hundreds of miles to visit their church on a Sunday morning. Today, you can listen to every sermon they have preached whenever and wherever you want with the click of a button on your phone. This easy access is a great tool, but also a terrible temptation.

I believe one of the biggest temptation pastors face is the desire to be someone else—to try to be their favorite preacher. We can quickly envy the successful preaching of another. We can believe the lie that we have to exactly like this other pastor to be successful. Some of us may even rip off another pastor's sermon and pretend it is our own. We become a cheap imitation of them instead of the real us.

As much as imitation is flattery to other pastors, it is an insult to God. It is like saying, "God, you made this pastor better than you made me. So I'm not going to be who you made me. I'm going to be them instead."

It is also a sign of insecurity, because you think that you are somehow less than someone else.

I was reminded of this recently while reading about David and Goliath in 1 Samuel 17. You know the story.

David is about to face the giant, Goliath. He is sure of God's calling. He knows what he is supposed to do.

After convincing King Saul to allow him to charge into battle, David faces a pivotal moment—a decision that could have completely changed the outcome of the story as we know it.

"Then Saul clothed David with his armor. He put a helmet of bronze on his head and clothed him with a coat of mail, and David strapped his sword over his armor. And he tried in vain to go, for he had not tested them. Then David said to Saul, "I cannot go with these, for I have not tested them." So David put them off. Then he took his staff in his hand and chose five smooth stones from the brook and put them in his shepherd's pouch. His sling was in his hand, and he approached the Philistine." (1 Samuel 17:38-40, ESV)

Saul puts David in his armor. After all, Saul is the king. Saul is a mighty warrior. Saul is a man of great influence—a man other men dream to be.

On top of that, Saul has the finest armor and the best sword money can buy. Who wouldn't want to be like the mighty king Saul (at least before he went crazy)?

David tries on Saul's armor, but makes a shocking decision. Rather than taking the king's royal weapons and armor, David chooses to fight the giant with a stick and stones!

David could have imitated the great warrior-king Saul, but he remained faithful to the shepherd that he was. It was a shocking decision, but you can't argue with the results.

I can only imagine David charging into battle imitating Saul in the king's armor only to trip over himself and become a quick afternoon snack for Goliath.

Against all conventional wisdom and best practices of his day, David is more effective with his own weapons.

Don't Wear Saul's Armor

I meet so many young men who want to see God do mighty things in their ministry, but they are copying the "kings" of our day—the famous pastors, big-name preachers, and guys who speak at all the conferences.

I have no problems with these well-known pastors. In fact, I highly admire and respect most of them. I even listen to a lot of their preaching.

The problem comes when we try to emulate them. We will only become a cheap imitation of our preaching idols.

You are not _____ (insert name of your favorite preacher here).

God made you to be _____ (insert your name here).

Like David, all preachers will face the temptation to be somebody they aren't—somebody they perceive as greater than they are. But if you want to see God use you in amazing ways, stop trying to copy somebody else.

Learn from good preachers, yes. But don't become a cheap knockoff of them.

You have your own unique calling to your own unique community. God created you to be you at this time, in this place, and for His unique purpose.

Learn from David. Be who God created you to be. Don't try to fit some perceived mold. Find your own unique voice.

If you try to copy another preacher, you will fall short. You won't fool anybody. You will be just another cheap imitation. A fake.

Your ministry may even fall apart like a pair of fake Oakley sunglasses.

Be yourself while remaining faithful to God's specific calling for you.

Preach Like No One Else

I'm weird. Most of the time, when driving my car, I'm not listening to top 40 radio I'm listening to a top 40 sermon. I just can't get enough of it. I love good preaching!

Now, I know I just wrote about the danger of imitating other preachers. However, there is a difference between imitation and inspiration. It's the difference between copying and learning.

Exposing myself to a lot of quality preaching has helped me grow as a communicator. They inspire me. Everyone who wants to improve should learn from those who are better than them.

This obsession only hurts me when I try to imitate one of my favorite preachers. I can get caught up trying so hard to preach like someone else that I no longer preach like me.

There is a fine line between inspiration and imitation.

Have you ever been there?

Think of how ironic this is. What do we love so much about all of our favorite preachers? Nobody else preaches like them! They all have their own unique voice and their own unique style.

What all of the great preachers throughout history have in common is that they are all different. They use the unique personality—the unique voice—that God gave them.

None of them stand up on stage and try to rip off someone else's sermon. So why do think we will be more like them by doing something that they, themselves, do not do?

Every preacher needs to find their own voice.

When I was a kid, my youth pastor always used to say, "One of you may be the next Billy Graham." I understand what he meant by this, but I cannot help but think we don't need another Billy Graham. We need you. Your unique voice. Your unique God-given personality.

You are not Rick Warren, Billy Graham, or Charles Spurgeon. You are you.

Last time I checked, the only person we are supposed to be imitators of is Christ.

So stop ripping off sermons by your favorite pastor. Stop fantasizing about being in their shoes.

There are enough copycats and clones out there.

Whatever it takes, find your voice. Be yourself. Preach your guts out.

Then you too will preach like no one else.

As the great theologian Dr. Seuss once said, "Today you are you! That is truer than true! There is no one alive who is you-er than you!"[3]

---

[3] Dr. Seuss, *Happy Birthday To You!* (New York: Random House, 1959).

THE 7 STEP SERMON PREP METHOD

Now that we have covered the fundamentals, we can get to the actual work of writing a sermon.

Years ago, my wife and I had the opportunity to have our very first home built. We chose to build in a brand-new housing development. Working with the builder, we got to pick the floor plan, paint colors, options in the design, the tile, the carpet, the lot it was built on, and everything in between. It was an awesome experience.

If you have ever been involved in building a house, you know the process of watching the house take shape from a dirt lot to your dream home is almost as exciting as moving into the house.

Every week we would swing by the lot and watch the progress. We took pictures during each stage: pouring of the foundation, the wooden framing, hanging drywall, and eventually moving in.

Writing a sermon is a lot like building a house.

There are 7 different stages that the construction of a message must go through before completion.

I call this method 7 Step Sermon Prep. It is sermon preparation method I always use to write compelling messages.

If you follow these steps in order, you will have a great sermon ready to preach in no time.

7 Step Sermon Prep:

1. Pray

2. Study

3. Focus

4. Illustrate

5. Outline

6. Edit

7. Practice

The next seven chapters of this book will cover each of these steps in more detail.

You can also download the 7 Step Sermon Prep Checklist for FREE at ProPreacher.com/checklist. It is a simple one-page checklist that I use to remind myself to follow the 7 Steps for each sermon.

Download it, and put it on your desk or the desktop of your computer for reference.

Once you have done that, you are ready to move on to the first step.

The first step in the process of sermon preparation is always prayer.

STEP 1 - PRAY

"I would rather teach one man to pray than ten men to preach."
—Charles Spurgeon

The first step in writing a sermon is to pray.

I know, I'm as surprised as you are!

But before you tune me out because you have heard all this before, hang in there, because prayer is not something to be taken lightly.

Going back to the house analogy, one of the first things you must do when building a house is to connect to the infrastructure of the city. You have to lay water, sewage, gas, and power lines. Although this process is not very exciting to watch, connecting these lines is crucial.

You could build the most elaborate mansion on the most beautiful land, but without the infrastructure, the toilets won't flush. Appliances won't work. The heater and air-conditioner won't blow. You cannot shower. And you better stock up on firewood and flashlights because you can forget about any lights at night.

A house needs to be tapped into a power source.

Prayer is the way we tap into God—the source of power for our sermons.

Do you want to preach a message backed by the power of God? Do you want the Holy Spirit to show up and change lives? You better pray.

Long before you lay the foundation of your message, you need to start here.

Too many pastors preach without prayer. They get so busy during the week that they forget. Maybe they lift up a few of the same generic prayers that they say every week, but they don't wrestle with God.

"No learning can make up for the failure to pray. No earnestness, no diligence, no study, no gifts will supply its lack."
—E.M. Bounds[4]

Pastors can quickly become functional atheists because we put all the responsibility on ourselves to preach a great sermon. It becomes all about our talent, our ideas, our words, and our personality.

---

[4] E.M. Bounds, *E.M. Bounds on Prayer* (Peabody, MA: Hendrickson Publisher, 2006), 115.

May we never preach this way. May we never erase God from the equation of our sermon preparation because we think we have it covered.

Prayer is never a waste of time.

Prayer Is Productive

Being a pastor is incredibly stressful. Would you agree? In the constant busyness of ministry, it is easy to neglect time in prayer to God.

In fact, one of the biggest excuses I hear for a lack of regular prayer is, "I am too busy." How many times have you thought the same thing?

When we pray, we feel like we aren't getting anything done.

The irony of neglecting prayer because we are too busy is that prayer is the best way to handle our busyness. Aside from the obvious spiritual benefits, we neglect the physical benefits of prayer.

Many studies have shown that people who pray regularly have lower levels of stress, anxiety, and depression. So if you are constantly stressed about the amount of work you have, pray!

The Bible commands us to give our burdens to God:

"Cast all your anxiety on Him because He cares for you" (1 Peter 5:7, NIV).

In the midst of our increasingly noisy and chaotic lives, there is something powerful about hitting the pause button and spending time with God.

Prayer takes our focus off ourselves and our need to control everything, and puts the focus on God's ability to take care of everything we need.

A lack of a prayer life shows that we are too dependent upon our own power, and not resting in God's power.

If we try to do everything ourselves, we ought to be stressed out. The burden of pastoral ministry is more than we alone can bear.

Look at Jesus. Even He needed time away to pray.

"Jesus often withdrew to lonely places and prayed" (Luke 15:16, NIV).

If Jesus often needed to escape the stress and pressure of the crowds to pray, how much more do we need to?

This one of the reasons why beginning with prayer is so important. It helps us to calm down, release our anxiety, and focus on the task God has for us.

When we are less stressed and more focused, our productivity increases. We get more accomplished with God than we ever could without Him.

Pray Hard

"The prayer of a righteous person is powerful and effective" (James 5:16, NIV).

Pray. Pray hard. Pray often. Pray before you ever sit down and stare at the blank page and blinking cursor on your computer screen. Pray before you ever crack your Bible. And don't stop there.

Just because prayer is Step 1, doesn't mean it shouldn't continue throughout the entire sermon writing process.

If prayer is a challenge for you, try this: set a timer on your phone for 5 minutes. Then, get on your knees, close your eyes, slow your breathing, quiet your mind from all distractions, and beg God to help you prepare your message until the timer goes off.

At first 5 minutes may seem like forever, but as you practice, you may find that 5 minutes becomes too short. When that happens, set the timer longer.

However, you do it, Beg God to show up. Ask the Holy Spirit to speak through you. Ask for direction and guidance for your message. Ask God to reveal to you what He wants you to say. Plead for hearts to be softened. Beg for lives to be changed.

Any man who ever hopes to accomplished anything great for God must begin on his knees.

Prayer is how we connect our sermon to infinite supply of the all-powerful God.

Apart from God we can do nothing. He is a nuclear power plant waiting for us to tap in. He is a water main waiting to flood our ministry with fresh water. Let's tap in.

Plug into the source of all power.

Connect to the infrastructure.

Pray.

Then you will be mentally focused and spiritually empowered for the next step.

STEP 2 - STUDY

"The teacher's temptation is to use the Scripture like the drunk uses a street light: more for support than illumination."
—unknown

It's Tuesday morning. You are sitting at your desk staring at a white page with the pressure to come up with yet another amazing sermon.

Being a pastor is hard. You are expected to hit the ball out of the park every Sunday. And have you noticed how frequently Sunday comes?

Great preaching takes time and you have little time to spare.

In the attempt to be creative and original, one of the things many pastors will do first is to brainstorm. What would be a creative sermon series? What is a good title? What is a memorable illustration I could use? What have I seen other churches do?

STOP!

This is the worst way to begin writing a sermon. Many pastors start this way, and it's wrong. When you do this, you blow right past prayer, detour around Scripture, and start the creative process.

If prayer is the power supply (as we said in Step 1), then Scripture is the foundation.

The foundation of a house is unbelievably important. A good foundation over time will support the house. A bad foundation over time erodes and collapses a house.

A good foundation anchors the house and helps it weather any storm. This is what Jesus says in Matthew 7:24-27:

"Everyone then who hears these words of mine and does them will be like a wise man who built his house on the rock. And the rain fell, and the floods came, and the winds blew and beat on that house, but it did not fall, because it had been founded on the rock. And everyone who hears these words of mine and does not do them will be like a foolish man who built his house on the sand. And the rain fell, and the floods came, and the winds blew and beat against that house, and it fell, and great was the fall of it"
(Matthew 7:24-27, ESV).

Jesus is telling us that His word is a firm foundation. The Word of God—the Bible—is our foundation.

When people leave your church building, do you want them applying God's word or just your best advice to their life?

After praying fervently for God's help (Step 1), open your Bible and get a word from the Word (Step 2).

Too many pastors start a sermon with a "good" idea. We pull inspiration from a popular book. We get an idea from a cool video. We listen to our favorite preacher and borrow inspiration from them.

Then we find a passage of Scripture that fits with the "good" ideas we have.

In seminary, they call this eisegesis. Eisegesis is a very poor interpretation of Scripture because you are looking to fit your idea into what the Bible says.

Eisegesis literally means "to lead into."

When you start with an idea, you are forcing your presuppositions into the Bible. You already know what you want to say. You are just finding a passage of Scripture that you can make say what you want it to say.

As you may know, people can twist the Bible say just about anything when taken out of context.

Eisegesis is a dangerous approach that leads to faulty theology and all-around bad preaching.

The proper way to interpret Scripture is called exegesis. Exegesis begins with God's Word and then pulls the idea out of Scripture. It is the opposite of eisegesis.

Exegesis means, "to lead out of."

Think of it as if you are excavating a section of the Bible. You start with the passage of Scripture and dig, and dig, and dig until you find all the treasures it contains. All of your illustrations, topics, titles, and creative ideas should flow out of what the Bible already says.

Eisegesis starts by asking, "What do I want to say?"

Exegesis starts by asks, "What does Scripture say?"

Do you see the difference? Rather than cramming Scripture into your mold, let Scripture be the mold.

I don't care how creative or smart you are. Compared to God, you are a moron, and so am I.

"For the wisdom of this world is foolishness in God's sight" (1 Corinthians 3:19, NIV).

With exegesis, you have the inspired, inerrant Word if God. With eisegesis, you have your "great" idea.

Should we start with ourselves or with God? I'm picking God every single time. He tends to always win.

It is not our job as preachers to make cool new ideas fit into the Bible, but to show how amazing the timeless truth in the Bible already is.

Let the inerrant, eternal Word of God be your foundation.

How We Misuse Scripture

Are bad at sermon math?

No, I'm not talking about actual math. By sermon math, I mean applying some form of change on the Scripture you preach.

As you prepare your sermon, it is important not just to begin with Scripture, but to properly apply Scripture. There are four types of sermon math that you need to avoid.

Addition +

Addition happens in when you add your own opinions or thoughts onto the Bible as if it is a commandment.

For example, imagine you were to preach Ephesians 5:18.

"And do not get drunk with wine, for that is debauchery, but be filled with the Spirit"
(Ephesians 5:18, ESV).

Some pastors will preach this sermon and talk about how drinking alcohol is a sin. They will even tell their churches that good Christians never drink alcohol. But is that what this verse really says?

Ephesians 5:18 says, "do not get drunk." It doesn't say anything about how all consumption of alcohol is a sin, just drunkenness. Anything we add to the sin of drunkenness would only be our opinion.

It might be a good suggestion to abstain from alcohol, but we cannot prescribe it as a Biblical mandate for all Christians.

This is addition.

The Pharisees were great at this. They added hundreds of rules on top of the Bible.

Subtraction –

Subtraction happens when you subtract a section from the Bible because you either don't want to deal with it or wish it weren't in the Bible in the first place.

Subtraction can easily be excused as trying to make the sermon more "seeker friendly" or not trying to get bogged down in the details. However, this can be a dangerous practice when we begin to pick and choose what parts of Bible verses we preach.

For example, let's say I'm preaching John 3 about Jesus' conversation with Nicodemus. I would love to cover John 3:16, but I may be tempted skip over 3:18 because it is highly offensive.

"Whoever believes in him is not condemned, but whoever does not believe stands condemned already because they have not believed in the name of God's one and only Son" (John 3:18 NIV).

It is easy to preach, "Jesus loves you and wants to give you the gift of eternal life if you believe in Him."

It is offensive to preach, "If you don't believe in Jesus you are condemned to Hell."

Preaching the whole chapter, but skipping this verse is subtraction.

Please note that I am not saying that you can't preach John 3:16 in a sermon by itself. I am talking about picking and choosing verses in a larger body of text. I have preached many sermons where I used John 3:16 as a supporting text.

Most of the time, subtraction is cowardice. We omit a verse because we are afraid to handle tough subjects.

Division /

Division happens when we divide a text from its context.

This far too common in preaching. We find an inspirational verse and preach it without any thought to what the original author intended the verse to mean.

One verse I see commonly divided from its context is Jeremiah 29:11.

"For I know the plans I have for you,' declares the Lord, 'plans to prosper you and not to harm you, plans to give you hope and a future"
(Jeremiah 29:11, NIV).

What a great promise from God. That will preach. However, I rarely hear it mentioned that this verse comes after Jeremiah 29:10. God says in Jeremiah 29:10 that the Israelites will first be sentenced to exile in Babylon for 70 years!

70 years is a long time. Most of the people will not live long enough to see the end of the exile.

Preaching Jeremiah 29:11 saying, "God immediately makes your life better," is division. It is misleading.

It is more accurate to say, "Even though life is often extremely difficult and God sometimes allows bad things to happen to you, God still has a plan. There is still hope."

It is our job to teach people how to read the Bible in its full context. There are enough problems with Christians taking verses out of context. Please don't add to the problem.

Dividing the text from its context is almost always a recipe for bad theology.

Multiplication *

Multiplication happens when we take an issue and multiply it into a much bigger issue than it should be.

Multiplication most often happens when pastors preach about particular sins. For example, a pastor may go off on people who practice homosexuality—which the Bible does call sin.

Yet, by railing against this one sin and not others, a pastor is multiplying the severity of only this sin. This goes against 1 Corinthians 6:9-10, which puts sexual immorality, adultery, homosexuality, stealing, drunkenness, slander, and other sins all in the same boat.

Another example of multiplication is a pastor who preaches about the end-times and says that true Christians are premillennial (as opposed to postmillennial or amillennial). Although there are legitimate arguments for different views of end-times theology, these are minor issues that should not become a dividing line between true believers.

Be careful not to multiply a small part of Scripture into something bigger than it is intended to be.

How to Start With Scripture

So where do we start? How do we make Scripture the foundation?

Here are a few practical tips:

Start by selecting the main passage of Scripture that you will be preach from.

Read the text. Then read it again and again and again. I recommend at least seven times. While reading, write down notes of any observations you have. Note any key phrases or sections that are confusing.

Read at least a chapter or two before and a chapter or two after the text so you understand the context of the passage. Ask, "What did the original author intend this verse to mean?"

Now that you are very familiar with the passage and have made your own observations, you have permission to open commentaries, or any other study tool of your choosing. Using reference materials after you study on your own helps your observations be formed by Scripture first (exegesis) instead of other opinions (eisegesis).

Capture good notes on everything you learn and observe. Ask questions. Get answers. Do the research. Study hard. Gather more facts and information than you need.

Don't worry about gathering too much information. We will sort through it all later.

The goal in Step 2 is to become an expert on this single passage of Scripture.

Know it forward and back. Live with it awhile. Let it sink deep into your soul. Engrave the words to your brain, so this Scripture becomes the rock-solid foundation of your message.

Let Scripture Be Your Foundation

We have to understand that the only thing that makes our message any different from humanistic wisdom of Oprah or Dr. Phil, is the Bible!

The Bible must be the foundation of our message. It should underly everything we say and do. It isn't just something we throw in to make our self-help talk a sermon.

The Bible is the very Word of God that molds and shapes human hearts in supernatural ways that no other book in human history ever has or ever will.

Find a text. Mine it for ideas. Lay the foundation. Then, we will use what you have discovered in Step 3.

STEP 3 – FOCUS

"I have a conviction that no sermon is ready for preaching, not ready for writing out, until we can express its theme in a short, pregnant sentence as clear as a crystal. I find the getting of that sentence is the hardest, the most exacting, and the most fruitful labour in my study."
—J.H. Jowett[5]

When you are building a house, one of the most exciting days is when the wooden frame is put up.

When my wife and I built our first house, for the first two months, all of the work was done at ground level or below. There was nothing but a dirt lot, some wires, and a slab of concrete. Then, suddenly, the frame was up in a single day.

Our house had finally taken shape!

Although it was far from finished, we could now see more clearly what the house was going to be like. We could walk through the hallways and see the dimensions of each room.

---

[5] J.H. Jewett, *The Preacher: His Life and Work* (New York: Harper & Brothers, 1912), 133.

We could still see through walls, but we could easily imagine the final product. How exciting!

Again, preaching is much like this.

In Step 1 and 2, we connected the infrastructure and laid the foundation. We did a lot of work without much to show for it. But in Step 3, we see it all come together with the frame—the focus of the sermon.

Just like the wood sets the framework of the house, the focus—or the Big Idea—sets the framework of the sermon.

By "Big Idea" I mean the one thing, based on the Scripture studied in Step 2, that your listeners need to know when you are done preaching.

If you had to boil the entire sermon down to a sentence or two, what would you say? That is the Big Idea. Think of it as the entire sermon in a tweet, or the sermon in a sentence.

With the first two steps, all you have is prayer and some Bible verses. The sermon could take many shapes. The Big Idea sets the framework—the direction of your message.

Everything in your message should be based on the Big Idea. The goal of the sermon should be to show your audience where the Big Idea comes from in Scripture, why it matters, and how it applies to their life.

Instead of preaching a seven-point sermon where all the points touch on different topics, the Big Idea keeps you focused on a singular thought. It helps eliminate anything that brings clutter or confusion to the sermon by not focusing on the central idea of the text.

You may still have a handful of points depending on your style, but now they all hinge on the a single idea.

Laser Focused Preaching

"A sermon should be a bullet, not buckshot. Ideally each sermon is the explanation, interpretation, or application of a single dominant idea."
—Haddon Robinson[6]

Many preachers preach like a light bulb; they shine their ideas in every direction and illuminate as much as possible. But the best preachers are like a laser; they focus intensely on a single idea until it pierces the heart.

The light bulb approach to preaching leaves the audience confused. They may walk away thinking you are really smart because of all the info you spouted. However, if you were to ask them what the message was about, they would not be able to give you a clear answer.

The best method is to keep it simple. Find the one idea that God wants your congregation to hear from His Word. Then hit it with all you got.

Take everything you learned in your study and boil it down.

---

[6] Haddon Robinson, *Biblical Preaching: The Development and Delivery of Expository Messages* (Grand Rapids: Baker Academic, 2001), 35.

Boil your paragraphs down into one memorable statement that will capture the singular, Big Idea of the message—a sermon in a sentence.

Stay focused.

The Big Idea keeps your preaching laser-focused on one big idea for a much greater a hundred little ideas.

It's time to put the light bulb away and pick up the laser. You won't cover as much content, but a single idea will penetrate far deeper into the hearts and minds of your congregation.

This might just be the game-changer your preaching needs.

How to Craft the Big Idea

In step 2, you did your homework. You now have a firm understanding of the Scripture that you will be preaching. You have read multiple translations. You consulted a few commentaries. You may have even done a Greek or Hebrew word study because you are scholarly like that.

Well done. You are now an expert on the text.

You should know what the main topic is. Maybe it's prayer, faith, or forgiveness. But the Big Idea goes further than just the topic. The Big idea summarizes the key idea or action point about that topic in a memorable way.

1. Summarize The Passage

The best way to begin to uncover the Big Idea in your sermon is to summarize the key passage of Scripture in your own words.

I like to work line-by-line and summarize each thought. This works great when preaching from a one of Paul's letters or wisdom literature when the author is simply explaining ideas.

However, when preaching a text like a narrative, the ideas may be a little more difficult to find. When I get stuck, I ask the following question: Based on the key passage, how should my audience think, act, or feel different?

After summarizing the passage or answering this question, you will probably have a paragraph or two. That's alright. You are heading in the right direction.

2. Narrow the Summary into a Memorable Phrase

The second step is to summarize everything in one memorable phrase. Something catchy. Something people will be able to carry with them throughout the week.

Your audience may not all be able to quote the Scripture you preach, but they can remember a catchy phrase. If it is short and memorable, people can bring it with them.

Before you reject this idea, don't forget about Jesus. Jesus was the master of memorable statements.

Think about some of Jesus' Big Idea phrases:

- "Do to others as you would have them to do you" (Luke 6:31).

- "Love your neighbor as yourself" (Mark 12:31).

- "No one can serve two masters" (Matthew 6:24).

- "Do not worry about tomorrow, for tomorrow will worry about itself" (Matthew 6:34).

- "What good will it be for someone to gain the whole world, yet forfeit their soul?" (Matthew 16:26)

- "Do not judge, or you too will be judged" (Matthew 7:1).

This list could go on. The point is, Jesus used memorable phrases that we still easily recall today.

These statements summarize a profound truth in a simple sentence. That is what we are aiming for with the Big Idea.

Example of Crafting a Big Idea

Let's look at how this process works.

The following is an example from a sermon I preached:

> **Scripture**: 1 Timothy 6:17-19 (NIV)
>
> "17 Command those who are rich in this present world not to be arrogant nor to put their hope in wealth, which

is so uncertain, but to put their hope in God, who richly provides us with everything for our enjoyment.
18 Command them to do good, to be rich in good deeds, and to be generous and willing to share. 19 In this way they will lay up treasure for themselves as a firm foundation for the coming age, so that they may take hold of the life that is truly life."

Here's how I summarized this passage:

> **Summary**: We are rich. God has blessed us with all we have for our joy (v.17). But with blessing comes responsibility to be generous and share with others (v. 18). Doing this not only builds treasure in heaven, but helps us live the best life possible today (v.19).

Then, I narrowed the summary into this memorable phrase:

> **Big Idea**: We are blessed to be a blessing.

Have you heard this phrase before? Maybe, but that's OK.

The Big Idea doesn't have to be original. It just has to be memorable. Many times, a direct quote from the Scripture is all you need.

I loved this phrase because it has a double meaning that summarizes the text perfectly. When God blesses us, he wants us to bless others. In return, by blessing others, we also live a blessed life.

Simple. Memorable. It worked.

My entire sermon from the introduction to the conclusion was then laser focused around the framework of this principle. I repeated this phrase as much as possible throughout the message so it would be burned into the memories of my audience.

Do you see now why a Big Idea is like the frame of a house? It gives you the framework of what shape your message will take.

Without this focal point, my sermon could easily get sidetracked. I could start rambling about any number of secondary issues related to money.

What's Next?

At this point, you have prayed to connected to the power source (Step 1). You have studied Scripture to lay the foundation (Step 2). You have focused on the Big Idea that will be the framework for your message (Step 3).

But the house isn't finished yet. It is still just a shell.

In Step 4 we will begin to fill out your message.

STEP 4 – ILLUSTRATE

"He did not say anything to them without using a parable" (Mark 4:34, NIV).

My wife's favorite part of building our first home was the day we went to visit the design center. The design center features a nearly unlimited selection of tile, carpet, countertops, cabinets, and more.

It was our job to walk through and pick out all of our favorite options for our new house. Large tile, small tile, or wood floors? Granite, Corian, or laminate countertops? What kind of cabinets? What light fixtures? White, brown, or blue carpet? You like brown carpet. Here are 47 shades of brown to choose from.

The design center took forever. My wife loved it. I got a headache. However, in the end, we finally walked away with exactly what we wanted.

This step was important. The layout of the house was already set, but the choices at the design center were going to change everything about the overall look and feel of the house. It was worth the effort to find what worked best for us.

Choosing illustrations for a sermon is similar to choosing the design for a house. Illustrations affect the overall look and feel of your message.

The difficult part is that there are nearly unlimited options. It is your job to painstakingly select the illustrations that work best for your message.

Most people think of illustrations as stories, but illustrations can be any creative element—videos, pictures, props, art, or music.

If you look up "illustrate" in a thesaurus, you will see that a synonym of the word is "decorate."

Although illustrations will not change the foundation of Scripture (Step 2), or the framework of the Big Idea (Step 3), they decorate the message. They make all the difference in how the audience connects with the sermon.

A good illustration compliments the sermon. It is a beautiful work of art that provides clarity, inspires action, or brings the message to life.

A bad illustration clashes with the sermon. It is an eyesore that confuses, distracts, or lessens the impact of the message.

What Makes a Good Illustration?

Have you ever used an illustration that you originally thought was good but it fell flat when you preached it? I know I have!

Why do some illustrations connect, while others fall short? What makes a good illustration?

The best sermon illustrations are founded on common ground between the speaker and the audience. When you speak about something you have experienced and your audience has also experienced the same thing, you connect with them on the deepest level.

A joke about something they all have experienced will make them laugh. An emotional story about something close to their hearts will bring them to tears. They will listen to you and think, "This is a down to earth pastor." Or "This guy gets me."

Haddon Robinson has a great diagram in his book *Biblical Preaching* to illustrate this concept. It looks something like the following:

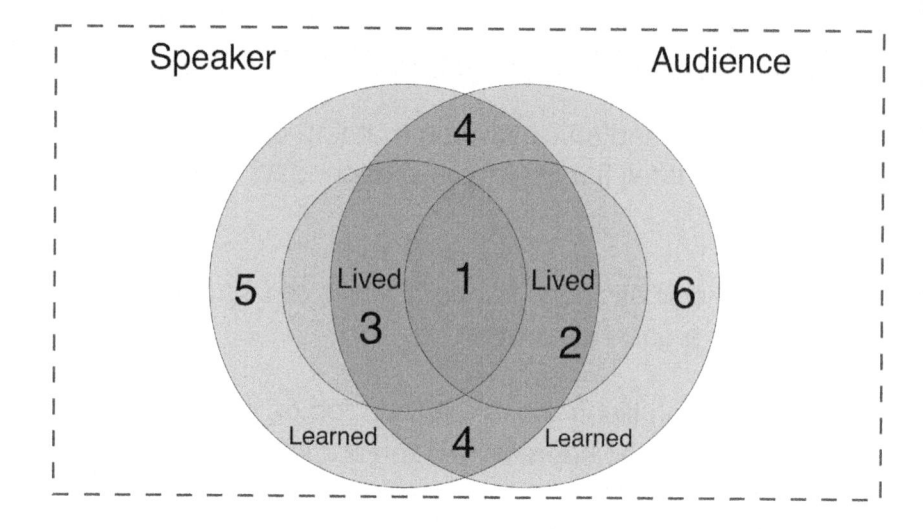

[Diagram: Venn diagram with Speaker and Audience circles, each containing Lived and Learned sub-circles, with regions numbered 1–6]

There are two kinds of experience that people have—Learned experience and Lived experience.

Level 1: The best illustrations connect on lived experience. You and your audience shared the same experience.

Level 2: Second best is when your learned experience connects with their lived experience. The audience has personally experienced what you are talking about.

Level 3: Third best is when your lived experience overlaps their learned experience. You experienced something your audience has heard about.

Level 4: Fourth is when both of your learned experiences overlap. You and the audience have heard about it.

Level 5: Fifth is when your learned experience doesn't connect with their lived or learned experiences. These illustrations hurt your message because they fail to connect with the audience.

Level 6: The worst illustrations of all are when you have neither lived nor learned about what they have learned about. You don't know what you are talking about, and the audience knows it!

When I was younger, whenever I heard a pastor tell a heart-warming story about a little girl, I wondered why people in the audience would cry. I would think, "What a bunch of emotional babies. Pull it together. It's just a story!" This was because stories about little girls were only a level 3 illustration for me. I did not fully understand.

However, after I became a father of a little girl of my own, suddenly these stories hit me emotionally too. When did I suddenly become such a crybaby?

Today, illustrations about little girls are a level 1 for me. They hit home. I can imagine my daughter in the place of the girl in the story.

Illustrations that connect on lived experience are always more powerful than anything else.

When you know your audience, you can find illustrations that hit home.

How should this impact your preaching?

Personal stories are often the best stories. If you have anything in common with your audience, there is a good chance that many of them have experienced similar things that you have.

Preacher stories from an illustration book might connect with your audiences lived experiences or learned experiences, but they don't always. So the next time you are tempted to tell a story about World War II, ask yourself how many World War II veterans will be in attendance? You may need a new story. Make sure it connects.

The key is knowing your audience. Are they rich or poor? Urban, suburban, or rural? Young singles, married couples with kids, or empty nesters? High school diploma, bachelor's degree, or masters? What are their careers? What are their biggest fears, temptations, and struggles?

When you know your audience, you will know which illustrations will connect.

Do this: Think about your audience and use this diagram to evaluate the illustrations for your next sermon. Try to find Level 1 illustrations first. If you cannot find a Level 1 illustration, then move down to Level 2 and so on.

Never, ever, ever use a Level 5 or Level 6 illustration, ever. Just don't. You are better off skipping the story.

This might just be the game-changer your sermon needs to better connect with your audience.

Why You Should Tell More Stories

The greatest reason you should tell stories is because Jesus told stories.

As you are probably aware, Jesus told countless parables. He pulled spiritual truths from everyday life. Not only did these stories make his teaching more memorable, but they also connected in a much more profound way.

Think about the parable of the Prodigal Son. Jesus could have taught, "God loves you so much that He will welcome you back no matter how sinful you have lived."

Instead, Jesus tells the story of a boy who disowned his family, partied away his inheritance, came home to beg for mercy, but was surprisingly welcomed with open arms by his father who waited daily for his return.

Which is more powerful?

Jesus used examples from everyday life to teach profound spiritual truths. I would argue that his parables were all either Level 1 or Level 2 illustration.

Think about it.

Most of Jesus' parables were agricultural, because he was speaking to people living in an agricultural society. He spoke to shepherds about sheep, and farmers about plants. He knew his audience.

If our mission in life is to be like Jesus, we ought to preach like Him too.

Other reasons to tell stories

- Stories connect emotionally, ideas connect intellectually. The most powerful sermons connect with people on both an emotional and intellectual level.

- Stories provide clarity to difficult concepts. Stories put skin on ideas, making them more tangible.

- Stories are memorable long after the sermon is forgotten. How many sermons do you remember from other pastors? How many stories? People naturally recall stories easier than points.

- Stories make hard truths easier to swallow. They can be like the sugar coating on a bitter pill. People are more receptive to tough teaching when they see how it plays out in a story.

- Stories capture our attention. Whether they are funny, exciting, sad, or inspiring, a well-placed story grabs an audience's wandering attention and thrusts it back to the message.

- Stories make a pastor human. When you share personal failures, funny moments, or hard times from your life, it shows that you are just like everyone else. It makes you more relatable. It also shows you believe what you are preaching and are trying to live it out as best as you can.

- Stories allow for easier application. I can tell you to be a good parent, but what exactly does that mean? A story can show what you mean in a very specific life situation.

Illustration Tips

As you think about what illustrations to include in your sermon, keep the following tips in mind.

Note: I will go much more in-depth with many of these tips later in this book in the "Creating an Illustration Database" chapter.

Look inward before outward.

Before you immediately jump online and Google "sermon illustrations," think about your personal stories and life experiences. What in your life, either in the past or present, could relate to the point of this message?

Your personal stories are entirely original to you. It is something that only you can tell.

Do you need a little help with this? I highly recommend doing a personal story mind map. This is an excellent way to dig thousands of illustrations from your life.

Collect more than you need.

Don't settle on the first illustration you think of, find in a book, or pull from the internet. Collect more than you need.

Gather as many good illustrations on your particular topic as you can without a second thought. Once you have collected all that you can find, the best ones for your particular sermon will rise to the top.

Select the best and toss the rest.

Think outside the box.

Illustrations are more than stories. Think through all the ways that you might be able to illustrate your idea. Then, pick the format that will be the most helpful or most interesting to your audience.

Are there videos you could use? Are there songs about your topic? Are there any photos or graphics that could help? Would it be helpful to draw your idea on a whiteboard? Are there any current events that relate? Are there any props you could use to demonstrate? What about quotes? Could you write your own parable to help?

Find illustrations before you need them.

Treat life as an illustration scavenger hunt. Always have a notebook or app ready to capture any illustrations you see.

Take pictures of things that are interesting. Keep a personal journal of unusual events of the week and what you learned from them. Save stories from articles, magazines, and books as you read them. Write down funny things your kids say. Record interesting things from your life. Whatever might work.

This is an exceptional discipline that will be a huge time-saver when you need to find a good illustration for a message. No need to panic, because you already ave a treasure trove of great ones to choose from.

Practice your delivery.

Sometimes an illustration sounds powerful in your head but fails when it leaves your mouth. Sometimes the problem is the story, but often the problem is the delivery.

Did you rush it? Did you pause effectively? Did your gestures add to what you were saying?

Your delivery is especially important when telling jokes. I cannot tell you the number of times I said something I thought was hilarious, that received no reaction from the audience. Sometimes the joke just wasn't funny to begin with, but many times the problem was in how I delivered it.

Work on it. Watch good comedians. They are masters at delivery. The more you practice, the better you will get, and the more your illustrations will connect.

Conclusion

Illustrations are one of the most powerful elements in your preaching arsenal. They add interest, creativity, personality, and memorability to your sermon.

Take your time in this part of the sermon preparation process to pick only the best illustrations. Then, we will finally have everything we need to piece together a great sermon in Step 5.

STEP 5 – OUTLINE

"The sermon outline should not just present data in an orderly way, nor just offer a "case" for a proposition. It should give people the sense they are being taken somewhere, building toward some kind of climax and finally being brought face-to-face with God."
—Tim Keller[7]

At this point in writing your sermon prep, you may be thinking, "I have done a lot of work up to this point without a lot to show for it."

Don't get discouraged. All the work done up until this point will make putting together your message much easier. In step 5, we will now assemble everything we have collected.

In the process of building a home, once the frame goes up and you have picked all the options at the design center, all that is left for you to do is wait while the construction crew finishes putting everything together.

---

[7] Timothy Keller, *Preaching: Communicating Faith in an Age of Skepticism* (New York: Viking, 2015), 225.

It is very exciting to watch everything come together. Every day something new is finished. Drywall. Windows. Paint. Tile. Carpet. Everything gets put in place, and before you know it, you have a completed house!

The outline process of writing a sermon is the same way. You already have your foundation of Scripture (Step 2), the Big Idea framework (Step 3), and the perfect illustrations (Step 4). These are your materials. Now it's time to put these elements together to create an actual sermon.

Move your elements around like puzzle pieces until you find the best fit.

What should be in the introduction? Where would this illustration fit best? Do I need an illustration to clarify this point? What will go in the conclusion to drive the point home?

Open your word document and begin copying and pasting the various elements you have already collected into it.

If you are a more visual person, try writing different elements on note cards or sticky notes and arrange them on a table or cork board.

One notecard may be your main passage of Scripture. Another may be a supporting passage. Another may be a personal story. Another may be a video you found. Another may be an application you want to make. If you have multiple points, you may have an individual notecard for each point.

Get the idea?

A clear outline is essential to a clear message.

How to Outline

I find that it helps to begin with a basic skeleton of an outline. Different sermons require different forms. However, based on your style, you may have a basic structure you like to follow.

Start with a skeleton outline and add all the elements you have gathered. Then, use the outline to fill in the details.

I like writing a full manuscript to clarify my thoughts, but I preach from a very basic outline. But I know other pastors who preach from a full manuscript, and others who only ever write an outline.

You will hear some pastors champion one way or another as the best way. I disagree. Every preacher is unique. God wired each of us differently. Experiment with different forms and styles to find what works best for you.

Outline Forms

If you need a place to start finding what works best for you, here are some of the different outline formats I have seen.

The Classic

Intro: introductory remarks

Body: Scripture, observations, and application

Conclusion: closing remarks

Me, We, God, You, We

Andy Stanley introduced this outline in his book *Communicating for a Change*.

Me: Here is a problem I have or have had.

We: Here is how this problem affects all of us.

God: Here is what the Bible says about this problem.

You: You should do this (application).

We: What would happen if we all did this?[8]

Hook, Look, Book, Took

Hook: Start with a hook that grabs attention or identifies a problem.

Look: Look at your life. How does this problem affect you?

---

[8] Andy Stanley, *Communicating for a Change: Seven Keys to Irresistible Communication* (Colorado Springs: Multnomah, 2006), 120.

Book: Check out this book. What does the Bible have to say?

Took: What have you took away from this? How will you respond?

3 Points and a Poem

Intro: Introduce the message and the key passage of Scripture

Point 1: What is the first point? Illustrate and apply.

Point 2: What is the second point? Illustrate and apply.

Point 3: What is the third point? Illustrate and apply.

Conclusion: Read a poem, or use a powerful illustration to drive the Big Idea home.

Head, Heart, Hands

Head: Intellectual appeal. Start by unpacking a heady idea in Scripture.

Heart: Emotional appeal. Use stories and illustrations that touch the heart.

Hands: Physical appeal. Provide a challenge to apply the message by actually doing something.

Just Tell Them

Tell them what you are going to tell them: Introduce the main points if the message.

Tell them: Explain main points in more detail.

Tell them what you told them: Concluding summary of main points.

My Message Template

Hopefully some of these general outlines help. In case you need a little more, here is an example of a message template that I wrote a while back to help some of the staff at my church.

Series Title: Message Title
1/1/16

Scripture: John 3:16 *(key passage from Step 2)*
Big Idea: Sermon in a sentence. *(Step 3)*

INTRO

This section captures a person's attention and answers the basic question: Why should I listen to you? Like any good movie, the message needs conflict. Highlights a problem. Paint a picture of a tension that the people in the audience have in their lives and want to see resolved. Make it so compelling that they will wait eagerly as you reveal the solution found in Scripture.

TRUTH

You built tension in the intro; now reveal the truth—what the Bible says about that problem. This is the majority of the message. (observations from Step 2)

I like to designate Scripture as follows and in bold to help it stand out in the manuscript:

John 3:16 (NIV)
16 For God so loved the world that he gave his one and only Son, that whoever believes in him shall not perish but have eternal life.

Add any necessary observations, background information, or illustrations.

Add any points you wish to make.

APPLICATION

This is where you apply the truth from the Bible to the everyday lives of your audience. What does living this truth out look like? Use highly specific, practical examples.

When adding illustrations in any part of the outline, I like to highlight it to stand out like this:

[STORY: Story Title] Once upon a time…

[VIDEO: Video Title] Watch this video…

[PIC: Picture Title] Look at this picture...

Designate the kind of illustration, and the title to make it simple to see exactly where these elements are in the message. This is helpful for preaching from memory, an outline, or the manuscript.

CONCLUSION

This is where you land the message by summarizing the problem and repeating the solution. If it fits, save your most powerful illustration for the end to engrave the message to the audience's mind.

Drive the Big Idea home. Keep it short and focused. Repetition, repetition, repetition.

PRAY

Close in prayer. You can write your prayer here if that helps. Otherwise, leave this area blank and pray as God leads you.

Summary

At this point, you have prayed to connected to the power source (Step 1). You have studied Scripture to lay the foundation (Step 2). You have focused on the Big Idea that will be the framework for your message (Step 3). You have picked all illustrations to decorate the sermon (Step 4). And you have completed the outline or manuscript (Step 5).

You may think you are finished, but there are still two more steps.

These next steps are the difference makers between good and great preaching.

STEP 6 – EDIT

> "A preacher should have the skill to teach the unlearned simply, roundly, and plainly; for teaching is of more importance than exhorting."
> —Martin Luther[9]

The sixth step in writing a sermon is the final inspection—editing.

When you build a house, and everything is finished, there is still one more step before you are allowed to move in. If you builder is any good, they will have someone walk through the house and inspect everything.

They are checking electrical outlets, air conditioning, door locks, light bulbs, the foundation, finishing touches on paint... you get the idea.

Usually, the final inspection will uncover a few things that were missed or built poorly. These issues are noted and fixed before the house officially closes, ensuring that

---

[9] Quoted in D. Martyn Lloyd-Jones, *Preaching and Preachers* (Grand Rapids: Zondervan, 2011). 140.

everything is up to code and meets the construction company's standards.

Preparing a sermon is no different. Although you may feel like you are finished after Step 5, editing is crucial. I guarantee that there are problems you overlooked.

There will be sections you wrote that looked good at the time, but upon further inspection, don't fit. There will be illustrations you used that are too long, or unnecessary. There will also be plenty of typos, punctuation, and spelling mistakes.

The benefits of editing your sermon are huge.

Benefits of Editing

Clearer – Your sermon will be clearer. How many times have you listened to a sermon and thought, "I have no idea where this guy is going right now." Good editing will remove everything that distracts from the primary focus discovered in Step 3.

Sharper – Your illustrations will be sharper. You will be able to cut all the unnecessary details to make a strong point. Editing will eliminate the fluff to make your words and sermon sharper.

Shorter – Your message will be shorter. You may find that 1/3 of what you originally wrote is unnecessary to your message. You can delete it, and it still makes sense. Good editing will reduce what you have written to nothing but the essential content.

When you cut the fat to get to the meat, a byproduct will be a shorter message. Nobody will complain about this. In fact, most people like shorter messages. (Note: Shorter doesn't mean less powerful or effective. Less is more when edited well.)

Stickier – Your teaching will be stickier. The words you say will stick with people longer because it is easier to remember focused teaching than scattered thoughts. Remember, laser-focused preaching leaves a lasting impression.

Better – Your preaching will be better. Editing your sermon not only helps you polish what you want to say, but the process is also beneficial for internalizing the message before you deliver it. Your delivery will be better because you know your message inside and out.

How to Edit a Sermon

How should you edit your sermon?

Walk Away

Before you begin the editing phase, let your message sit for a while. When you are able to walk away from a message for a few hours or days, you will find that you will be able to look at the message again with a fresh set of eyes.

Clear your head. Take a break. Go for a walk. Sleep on it. Pray. Go for a lunch or coffee break. Do whatever you need to do to get out of sermon writing mode for a while so you can come back with fresh eyes, ready to go.

Stepping away will help you be less attached to the words you wrote and more objective about what stays and what goes.

Mark It Up

When I edit, I print out my manuscript, pull out a sharpie, and mark up my sermon like a madman.

You may be fine editing just the word document. But I find that there is something magical about holding the manuscript in your hand and using a physical marker/pen to edit it. I feel like I can look at my sermon from a different perspective on paper than on a screen.

As you read through your manuscript ruthlessly, cut everything that is not necessary. Every run-on sentence. Every tangent. Every thought, fact, or idea that does not contribute to the Big Idea. Every illustration that is unnecessary or confusing.

Make sure that the Big Idea is clear. Check to ensure that you are staying true to Scripture in every thought.

Imagine yourself preaching the message on stage. Then, reword sentences more like you would say them in a conversation, instead of a term paper.

Evaluate your the application points to ensure they are hitting real things your audience faces day to day.

Try putting yourself in the shoes of people in the congregation. Ask what would Phil think about this? How might Jane object to this thought? (As suggested in the "Know Your Audience" chapter)

Cross out entire paragraphs. Circle others and drawing arrows to where they need to be moved. Fill the margins with thoughts, ideas, sentences that you want to add, or facts you need to research further.

When I edit, I am also editing for grammar, spelling, and punctuation. Grammar mistakes and typos drive me crazy. After the first draft, my manuscripts are filled with them.

By the time I am done editing, my manuscript is destroyed. Where I may have started with eight pages, I am usually down to four. This may seem like a lot of work, but the four pages I have left are pure meat after cutting four pages of fat.

Put It Back Together

Now get back on the computer and piece your sermon back together.

Delete everything you crossed out. Make the changes you marked.

In this stage, I typically still catch a few more things that I missed earlier.

Once all the changes have been made, everything should be polished. The message is clear. The points are refined. You should feel pretty darn good about the work you have done.

Check Your Word Count (Optional)

Nothing feels worse than having a great sermon prepared, then realizing on stage that you are almost out of time and only half-done preaching.

A great tip I learned from a friend is to find the average words per minute that you typically preach. Once you have calculated this, you know roughly how many words you need to write to fit your given time allotment, and, more importantly, when you have way too much content.

Listen to a recording of yourself preaching. Get out a stopwatch and count every word for 60 seconds. Do this three times at different spots in the message if you want a better average.

Many people speak faster in an introduction because of nerves, and slower in the middle as they get comfortable.

I speak roughly 100 words per minutes. Therefore, for a 30-minute sermon, I want a manuscript of around 3,000 words. This isn't an exact science. Sometimes I speed up, slow down, or go off script and say something unplanned.

In fact, I don't ever preach my manuscript word for word. It is more of a guide for me. However, checking my word count has been a huge help because I practice with my manuscript.

Don't get too caught up in word count, but try it out.

Calculate your average number of words per minute. Set a word count goal for your message. Then stick to it within a hundred words or so. You will be surprised by how accurate this is.

Almost Done!

You might be thinking, "Wait, isn't the sermon finally done now? I wrote everything. I edited ruthlessly. My outline is perfect. My manuscript is polished. I have put in a lot of work on this thing. What else could I possibly do?"

Many pastors stop here. But I firmly believe that Step 7 makes perhaps the biggest difference between an average preacher and a great one.

STEP 7 – PRACTICE

"Practice isn't the thing you do once you are good. It's the thing you do that makes you good."
— *Malcolm Gladwell*[10]

When building a house, the process doesn't end the day they hand you the keys. After you move in, there is still a warranty period.

Even with the inspections and a quality effort by the construction crew, something will inevitably go wrong after you move in.

For my house, there were a few problems. Some of the windows were not properly sealed. After the first rain storm, condensation built up in the windows. Also, as the foundation settled, some of the drywall developed hairline cracks.

---

[10] Malcolm Gladwell, *Outliers: The Story of Success* (New York: Little, Brown and Company, 2008), 42.

None of these things could have been detected without time living in the house.

Fortunately, we had the warranty! I just called the warranty department, and they fixed everything free of charge. You have to love a good warranty!

What does this have to do with your sermon?

Step 7 in writing a sermon is to practice—move in.

Running through your sermon is like the new home warranty. After you have gone through the previous six steps, your message looks, smells, and feels finished—like a new home. But when you live in your sermon for a while and practice it a few times, you begin to see the cracks.

Practicing is like a warranty; it lets you fix problems before you pay.

Many pastors are tempted to skip practice because it takes a time and can be repetitive. Don't get lazy!

Practicing your sermon is one of the biggest difference makers between being an average preacher and a great one.

Why You Need to Practice Your Sermon

A sermon is much different on paper than spoken. Not everything will translate off the page to your lips.

You will catch things you missed in the editing process.

You will learn how to deliver different parts of the message better. You can work out the best tone, volume, pace, gestures, pauses, eye contact, facial expressions, or even sound effects.

The Holy Spirit will inspire changes. Ideas will pop into your head that work even better than what you have written—a perfect illustration, a conversation you had, a joke, or a way of seeing the Scripture that you have never seen before. Often my greatest moments of clarity and inspiration come in this final stage of preparation.

The better you know your message, the more confident you will be delivering it. There is nothing more terrifying than standing on stage with everyone watching you and not knowing what to say next. Seriously, I have recurring nightmares about standing to preach and forgetting everything I planned to say. Practicing ensures that this does not happen.

Besides, you will get better at preaching overall. You are not just working to get better at one sermon. Every time you practice, you are becoming a better preacher for every future sermon too!

Practice won't make perfect. There is no such thing as a perfect sermon. But practice will definitely make you better.

Ways to Practice a Sermon

- Read your message out loud.

- Practice with notes.

- Practice without notes to see how much you remember.

- Practice on the stage you will preach on.

- Practice in front of the mirror to watch your body language, gestures, and eye contact.

- Practice in front of a few people to get feedback.

- Practice with a coach or mentor to critique you and offer advice.

- Practice in front of a camera so you can watch yourself and make corrections.

How I Practice My Sermons

After my manuscript is complete, there is a basic rehearsal process that I like to implement the night before I preach.

Like my editing process in Step 6, I like to print out the manuscript of the message. Then, I get alone in a room away from everyone so I can practice, fail, and feel stupid without anyone noticing.

I also like to time each run-through with the timer on my phone so I know roughly how long the message will be and if I need to shorten it.

First, I read the entire message word for word out loud. As I'm reading, I have a pen ready to scribble any changes that I think need to be made.

Second, I read the entire message out loud again while trying to look less down at the paper and more up at my imaginary audience.

Third, now that I am feeling a little more confident, I put the manuscript down and practice preaching the message as best I can without looking at all (except when reading Scripture). I usually stumble with words, forget my place, and have to stop and look at the message a lot. However, I am always surprised by how much I already know at this point.

Then, I edit together my final outline with any changes I noted while rehearsing. Although I rehearse with a manuscript, I only carry a minimal one-page outline on stage.

Sticking to only one page forces me to cut everything except for the Scripture I will read, a few key points, and cues for illustrations, pictures, or videos.

Finally, on Saturday night, I read my manuscript a few times then lock myself in my closet (I'll explain later) to practice my entire message a few times just using my outline.

I never feel fully prepared, but eventually, I have to call it a night so I can get some sleep before church in the morning.

The morning of the sermon, I don't have time to practice alone, so I continually run through my sermon in my head and pray over it while getting ready, driving to church, and getting set up.

Here's the point: I preach a lot of bad sermons to an audience of nobody, so when I am in front of somebody, I am ready to go.

That is what it looks like for me. Take what you can, but find a routine that works best for you. Every pastor prepares a little different.

Warning: As beneficial as practice can be, it is possible to practice too much. At some point, there is a diminishing return on your practice. Do not practice so much that you become robotic. Find what works best for you to internalize the message and be confident while still allowing for a natural delivery.

Remember this: You will never preach a perfect sermon, but you do have a perfect God, who will use your imperfect message to accomplish His perfect mission.

Do your absolute best and God will handle the rest.

Preach to the Coats

I am a closet preacher. I literally practice preaching in a closet.

My wife makes fun of me.

As newlyweds, we lived in the smallest, ugliest one bedroom apartment on earth. It was old, falling apart, and had the grossest blue carpet you have ever seen. The blue carpet was so worn that it was flat in the middle of the room but fluffy and a good inch taller around the walls.

Since there was no space, I had nowhere to rehearse my sermons in private.

I was too nervous to practice in front of my wife. The only place I found to get away was our closet. I would go into the closet, shut the door, and preach to the coats.

Without fail, every time I finish practicing, my wife says, "So, you finally decided to come out of the closet." She laughs. I shake my head. That's the routine.

Since I am a creature of habit, this weird routine stuck. I still practice every sermon in our closet, even though we now have a lot more space in our house.

But here is one thing I have learned: If you want to preach like great preachers, you have to prepare like them.

Before I got into full-time ministry, I remember picking up the autobiography of Billy Graham, *Just As I Am*. Before he was a famous preacher and evangelist, Billy would go out into nature and practice preaching to animals and trees.

That picture of young Billy Graham preaching to trees stuck with me. Billy Graham put in the work. He wasn't born a natural preacher. In fact, he even wrote about how terrible his first sermons were. But while other people were out doing normal things, Billy was preaching to trees.

When nobody was watching, Billy was getting better. He was honing his craft. He was doing the time.

In his book, *Outliers: The Story of Success*, Malcolm Gladwell writes about the 10,000-hour rule. The rule basically says that it takes around 10,000 hours of practice before somebody becomes an expert at something. He found this to be true anywhere from professional hockey players to Bill Gates.

The reason people are successful is not always that they are more talented than everyone else. More often than not it is because they took the opportunity to put in more time.

Billy Graham got his hours in early, and it paid off.

Therefore, as weird as my habit of preaching to coats is, I am convinced I am not crazy. I am getting in my hours. I am doing the work it takes to get better at my craft.

If you want the most out of your preaching, you have to put in the time.

Do the work.

Log the hours.

Practice, practice, practice.

It doesn't matter if you are preaching to trees, coats, stuffed animals, or a mirror. Keep practicing. Keep working on it. Keep seeking God's help.

Don't settle on thinking you can get by on talent alone, or fall into the trap of thinking you are not talented enough.

If you have the fire inside you to preach, put in the hours.

You may not see results immediately, but over time practice always pays off.

HOW TO GET AHEAD ON SERMON PREP

If you have made it this far and applied all 7 Steps, congratulations! You wrote a great sermon!

But... Sundays come with terrifying regularity.

Coming up with a new sermon to preach every single week is one of the most stressful aspects of preaching.

Let's take a test. Do any of the following points describe you?

- You are continually worried about what you are going to preach next.

- You often find yourself pulling out a Saturday night special (finishing your sermon just before you preach it).

- Nobody in your church knows what you are preaching about next (staff included).

- You have nightmares about standing on stage and having nothing to say.

- You often feel overwhelmed.

- You feel like your sermons are stale—like you keep preaching about the same things, or you have run out of creative ideas.

- You feel like you never have enough time to work on your messages.

If any of the above descriptions describe you, you need to get ahead on your sermon preparation.

Yes, it is possible. This chapter will show you how.

Why You Need to Get Ahead

I cannot overstate the benefits of getting ahead on sermon preparation.

Here are a few:

Knowing what you are preaching in advance eliminates stress.

When you have your preaching calendar laid out, you no longer have to panic every Monday about what you are preaching about Sunday. You already decided the schedule.

When a crisis pops up —you have to make an emergency hospital visit, preach a sudden funeral, or get the flu—it's no problem.

You don't have to stress that your week is over, and you haven't had time to work on your message. You already have your message written!

Knowing what you are preaching in advance gives the sermon time to marinate.

If you know that you are preaching Ephesians 5-6 about marriage in a few month, you will be more alert when ideas and illustrations present themselves.

If you have a silly argument with your wife that could make a great story, you will write it down knowing you will need it. If you come across a great article, you can set it aside to be used later.

Simply make a folder on your computer for each message you will be preaching. Then, when you come across an article, illustration, picture, or video you can store it away. Now, when it is time to knock out that sermon, you already have the research and illustrations waiting for you to pick the best.

This simple discipline is a game changer. We will talk more about it in the next chapter.

Knowing what you are preaching in advance saves you time.

Less stress makes you happier and more productive. Being more productive gives you more time to read and study in advance.

Plus, capturing ideas and stories as they come to you in your daily life saves hours of study time.

Knowing what you are preaching in advance allows your creative team to do their best work.

Having your messages laid out in advance allows you to organize a volunteer team that takes your sermon and creates art, video, music, stage designs, or whatever to back it up. You cannot do this if you are preparing sermons week to week.

Even if you have a paid creative team, this also gives them time to do their best work. Videos, graphics, and worship sets that they have months to work on will always be better than if they are rushed.

You will also have enough time in advance to create group materials or other resources to coincide with each series.

How to Create a Preaching Calendar

The first place to start, as always, is seeking the inspiration of the Holy Spirit in prayer. I am assuming by now that you already know to do this. So let's focus on the practical side of planning.

I have worked with a lot of amazing pastors, and I learned quickly that the way all good preachers get ahead is by laying out a preaching calendar.

A preaching calendar doesn't have to be anything fancy. A paper annual calendar or a spreadsheet on your computer will do. I like using a large whiteboard to get the process started. Then, I record it digitally.

Here is an example of what a calendar spreadsheet might look like:

DATE	SERIES	SERMON TITLE	SCRIPTURE	SPEAKER	NOTES
Jan 5	God is…	Immutable - Unchanging	Psalm 102:25-27		
Jan 12	"	Omnipotent - All Power	Jeremiah 32:17		
Jan 19	"	Omniscient - All Knowledge	1 John 3:20		
Jan 26	"	Omnipresent - All Places	Psalm 139:7-12	Guest	

DATE	SERIES	SERMON TITLE	SCRIPTURE	SPEAKER	NOTES
Feb 2	Book of James	Testing Your Faith	James 1:1-18		
Feb 9	"	Hearing + Doing	James 1:19-27		
Feb 16	"	Don't Play Favorites	James 2:1-13		
Feb 23	"	Faith + Works	James 2:14-26		
Mar 2	"	Taming the Tongue	James 3:1-12		
Mar 9	"	Wisdom from Above	James 3:13-18		
Mar 16	"	War on Worldliness	James 4:1-12		
Mar 23	"	Tomorrow is No Guarantee	James 4:13-17		
Mar 30	"	Warning to the Rich	James 5:1-6	Guest	
Apr 6	"	Patient Suffering	James 5:7-12		
Apr 13	"	Persistent Prayer	James 5:13-20		
Apr 20	Easter	The Resurrection	Luke 24:1-35		

Remember, your preaching calendar isn't like the Ten Commandments; it's not written in stone. It can be adjusted as you go.

Think of the calendar as a roadmap. It is a tool to help guide you, but every road trip occasionally has a detour.

Whatever tool you use, make sure there is enough room.

There are 52 weeks in a year. If you preach once a week, that means you need 52 sermons. If you preach twice a week, you will need 104 sermons. Find the date for each of these sermons, and mark them down. This is your calendar.

Once you have your calendar ready, start by filling in the big days first.

Look at holidays and special Sundays

Add all the big events and holidays to your calendar: Christmas, Easter, Mother's Day, Father's Day, Memorial Day weekend, and any other special Sundays.

What impact will these days have on your preaching? Obviously, Christmas and Easter are big ones, but what about other special weekends?

Look at special days in your community

Every city is different. Are there any special events in your community that might affect your preaching?

Some events you can ignore, some you can leverage, and others you are better off not fighting.

For example, when I served at a large church in Albuquerque, New Mexico, every October it was Balloon Fiesta time. Balloon Fiesta is the biggest gathering of hot air balloons in the world. Hundreds of balloons take flight every morning at the same time and fill the sky. It is a remarkable sight to see. And, consequently, church attendance always dropped on those weekends. We didn't fight it. Instead, we reserved our best material for another time.

How do the seasons affect your ministry? Do you get more or less visitors in the winter? Do people stick around for the summer or leave town? If you are in a college town, is your attendance affected by the school's semesters? Are there any unique festivals or celebrations in your community?

Decide what days you will preach

Determine how many weeks out of the 52 you are preaching.

What weekends do you plan to be on vacation? What days will you take a break so you can get ahead?

What days are you letting someone else preach for you? Are you allowing other staff members to speak? Are you bringing in any guest speakers?

If you plan on preaching every week, it is a sign that you are (A) a workaholic, (B) a control freak, and (C) setting your church up to fail if you ever resign or get hit by a bus.

Who are you developing? Healthy preachers share the platform to developed other communicators. Plan this on your calendar.

Plan your message series

Some pastors prefer walking verse-by-verse through entire books of the Bible; others only preach topical sermons.

Playing to your strengths is OK. However, I suggest a balanced approach using four different types of sermon series. Just remember that each should be thoroughly grounded in Scripture.

Bible – A Bible series is either preaching through an entire book of the Bible, or a digging deep into a select passage such as the Ten Commandments, the Beatitudes, or the Fruit of the Spirit.

Topical – A topical series is based on felt needs of your audience. What does Scripture say about things like marriage, money, parenting, or suffering? These are messages your audience needs to hear every year because these topics are the issues they face every day. Your time spent with your audience, counseling them, and knowing what they struggle with should help shape these sermons.

Vision – A vision series is focused on the vision, mission, or values of your church. Where are you going and how will you get there? What does your congregation need to do to advance the kingdom of God? These messages are about strategic topics like core values, small groups, evangelism, serving in a ministry, serving the community, and missions.

Special – A special series is either a stand-alone message or a series based on a special event or need. These kinds of sermons are common for days like Christmas, Easter,

Mother's Day, Father's Day, or when you have a guest speaker.

How to Plan an Entire Year of Preaching

Planning an entire year of sermons is no small task. It requires time and focus.

Try the following tips to keep from getting overwhelmed:

Get away

Chances are, you are not going to get a year of planning done in the office. You have too many distractions. So take a week to get away by yourself or with your team to plan out the entire year of preaching.

Turn off your phone. Don't check your email. Don't schedule any appointments. Don't let anyone bother you unless it's a serious emergency.

Studies have proven that setting aside a large portion of time to be singularly focused on one task will help you get more done in less time than if you multitask or break up your time.

Brainstorm

Allow other staff members or a select team of church members to be a part of your preaching team. Let them help you come up with sermon ideas.

Give your preaching team homework in advance. Tell them to bring specific ideas or resources with them to the meeting. Assigning homework in advance will allow the team to bring their best ideas to the table, and save you time during your meeting.

Throughout the year, keep a notebook or an app on your phone with you at all times so you can capture sermon ideas as they come to you. Build a deep reservoir of ideas. Then, when it comes time to lay out your calendar, you aren't starting from scratch. You can pull from a full year's worth of ideas.

Write two messages a week

I worked under an amazing pastor once who was two years ahead in his sermon writing! No, that wasn't a typo.

He was two years ahead. And I'm not just talking about planning the topics; I'm talking a full manuscript written for each sermon!

No joke. The man is a machine.

But how did he do it?

When I asked him, he responded, "I wrote two messages every week for years."

Try to wrap your mind around how that might feel. He could not write another sermon for the next two years, and he would be fine!

Now, I know that this is an extreme example, but it proves that it is possible.

You may not need to be two years out, but there's nothing stopping you from getting two or three months out.

Set a goal for how far out you want to be and go for it!

Once you are as far out as you want to be, this is easy to maintain. All you have to do every week is revisit the sermon you wrote for the current week and write one for the future.

The great thing is that the sermons you write for the future don't have to be flawless. Even if you only create the outline, just write them. You will refine and perfect them the week you preach them.

Get Started

Make it your goal this year to finally get ahead. Do whatever it takes. The weight of stress that will fall from your shoulders is worth it!

I learned this technique from the pastor I worked for, and I can almost guarantee you that your favorite preachers do something similar in their planning.

Don't make excuses.

The only thing stopping you from getting ahead is you.

Get disciplined. Start planning. You can get ahead. Your ministry and your life will be better for it.

CREATING AN ILLUSTRATION DATABASE

"All originality and no plagiarism makes for dull preaching."
—Charles Spurgeon

Building an illustration database is one of the best things you can do to save time during sermon prep, and make your sermons better.

This chapter will cover some of the tips and tricks to creating a stockpile of illustrations.

As a preacher, you should treat life like an illustration scavenger hunt. Always be on the lookout for a good illustration. Whether it's an article online, a story in a book, or something you experience, capture it immediately.

Don't trust your brain to recall them when you need them. I'm sure you are well aware of how limited your memory can be.

You need a place to store your illustrations so you always have an abundance to from choose whenever you need.

Before you embark to gather all of these illustrations, you need a system to organize them. There is no point saving illustrations if you can't find them when you need them.

Old school pastors used to use physical files and file cabinets. Today some pastors use a system of folders on their computer. However, my personal favorite is the Evernote app.

How I Use Evernote

Evernote is a free note-taking application that syncs all your notes onto your computer, phone, tablet, and online. You have easy access no matter where you are.

I like to think of it as my digital brain. It remembers everything for me, so I don't have to.

Imagine having every good sermon illustration you have ever read or used accessible at the click of a button. Evernote makes that possible.

If my kids say something funny, or I experience something interesting that could make a good illustration, I whip out my phone and write it down. If I read a great story online, I copy it to Evernote. If I hear a great quote, I save it in Evernote. If I see something that looks funny, I take a picture of it and save it into Evernote.

This next tip changed my life. I have switched from physical books to reading all of my books on Kindle for a trick that many people don't know about. If you go to kindle.amazon.com, you can pull up every highlight and note you ever made!

After I read a book, I copy all of my highlights and paste into Evernote.

Then, anytime I am doing research for a sermon, a quick search in Evernote will pull up all the relevant highlights from every book I have ever read!

I don't have to spend hours sifting through book after book looking for something that might be in it. Evernote does all this for me within seconds!

Yes, it takes a little bit of time on the front end getting all your notes in there, but getting all your book highlights and illustrations into Evernote will save you hours of research every week.

If it sounds like too much work, consider asking an assistant or volunteer help with the data entry.

If you still like reading physical books, highlight the book with a color code. For example yellow = statistic, blue = story, and green = quote. Or simply write it with a pen in the margins. Then a volunteer or assistant can help type and categorize your notes into Evernote for you.

In Evernote, I have a notebook I created called "Illustrations." Then, within that notebook, I have five different folders for each type of illustration I use.

1. **Illustrations** – In this folder, I save all general illustrations and stories from books, magazines, or websites.

2. **Personal Illustrations** – This folder is filled with stories from my life. Every story I have ever used is in this file, along with many others I have taken the time to write down for later (more on this soon).

3. **Visual Illustrations** – These are ideas that I have for a visual illustration or object lesson. For example, I have a note in this folder about a time I used a bag of potato chips to illustrate how sin works. I asked if anyone would like one, and gave a single chip to different people in the audience. After they had eaten it, I asked how many of them are craving another. Then, I explained how it is nearly impossible to eat just one. You have the desire, and give in, but the desire doesn't go away. You keep saying, "Just one more and then I will stop." Then, before you know it, you have eaten the entire bag. Sin begins with desire and continues to grow until it leads to death (James 1:14-15).

4. **Quotes** – You guessed it; this is where I store all my favorite quotes that I come across. A good quote now and then adds credibility to your sermon. I also find that

quotes can be a great source of inspiration for a particular topic when you have trouble finding the right words to say.

5. **Sermon Statements** – This is similar to quotes but slightly different. These are powerful one-liners that I might want to use. For example, I once heard a pastor talking about gossip say, "If you aren't an eye-witness, you are a false witness." I wrote it down and saved it for later. The next time I preach on gossip, I will use this line.

The great thing about an electronic database like Evernote is that in addition to notebook categories, it allows me to create "tags" for each note for other categories it fits. For example, I could tag an illustration with "heaven," "hell," "love," "marriage," "faith," or "temptation."

I may tag an illustration with five or six different tags because it fits more than one category. This way when I am preparing for a sermon about Heaven, I just have to click on the "Heaven" tag and every illustration with that tag in any folder will instantly appear.

Here's another helpful tip: write at the end of each illustration the date you last used it. This helps prevents you from unknowingly going back to your favorite illustrations too often. It also lets you know when it might be OK to reuse a good one.

Building Your Personal Illustration Library

If you Google "sermon illustrations," you will find thousands of them. I'm sure we have all done this before. However, most of these illustrations are just bad. They are old, outdated, and may not connect with your audience.

However, if you are in a bind and need some quality illustrations, I post new illustrations from my personal archive every week at ProPreacher.com that may be helpful to you.

But what if I told you that I could show you how to get access to thousands of the best illustrations that you won't find anywhere on the internet for free?

Are you interested?

As I wrote earlier (Step 4), the best illustrations, connect with both you and your audience's lived experiences (Level 1). Canned illustrations don't work as well as a personal story that your audience can relate to.

Therefore, the best way to get free sermon illustrations is to pull them from your own life.

You have to build up your personal illustration database. Take a long trip down memory lane and record every memorable experience you can think of. This takes a little work, but the stories you pull from your own life will be gold.

The best way I have found to do this is through creating a personal illustration timeline.

1. Map a Timeline of Your Life

Try this out. Get a blank piece of paper.

First, draw a stick figure in the center. This is you. You are looking good. Have you lost weight?

Now, start listing the major time periods or categories of your life. You might write things like childhood, middle school, high school, college, marriage, or kids.

You can go as general or as detailed as you like. For example, you could write "high school" or go further labeling each grade (9th, 10th, 11th, 12th grade) or each year.

For the example below, I went general, but the more specific, the better.

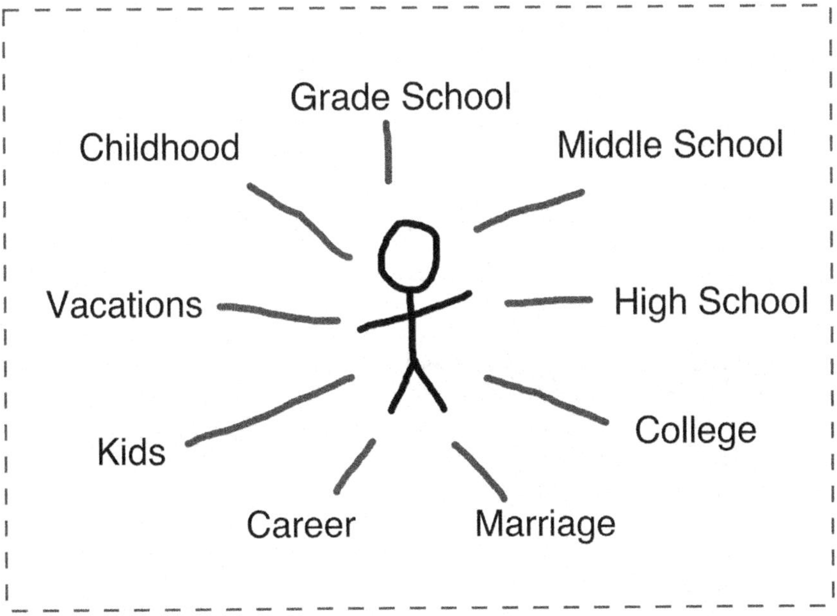
Grade School
Childhood
Middle School
Vacations
High School
Kids
College
Career
Marriage

2. Find Stories That Could Be Illustrations

Do you have all your categories? Great. Now go further in depth under each category. Walk through each period of your life and write down anything that comes to mind.

Don't over think it. Just brain dump anything that pops into your head.

Be on the lookout for things that make a good story—embarrassing moments, defining moments, shocking events, turning points, regrets, funny situations, and life lessons.

Think about the sports teams you played on, your first crush, your 2nd-grade teacher, the death of a favorite pet, getting grounded, awkward dates, family vacations, dumb decisions, and so on.

Take your time with this. You don't want to miss anything.

Here is one brief example from my life in middle school:

Middle School

- school dance
- cut from basketball
- bullies
- fight
- regrets
- funny moments
- teachers
- riding bus
- friends
- football champs

I went to some awkward school dances, was cut from the basketball team, had some bullies pick on me, and made many other great memories. This example is very general, so you will want to go deeper than this if you can. The more specific, the better.

3. Gather Details

Congratulations, if you took your time with this exercise, you now have a list of hundreds if not thousands of stories from your whole life!

Are you surprised how many stories you have? I was when I first did this. But hold on, you aren't done yet.

Get detailed. Write down some bullet points for each story of important details. Don't write the story word for word. That would take too long. You can do that when you decide to preach it. Just capture the main points to help jog your memory later.

For example, I was cut from the basketball team in 7th grade. It was one of the worst feelings in my life. But I worked hard and made the team in 8th grade. I even started my first game! Sadly, that was the only game I started. When I got the ball, I panicked. I don't know what I was thinking, but I launched an insane half-court shot. The coach benched me for the rest of the year. My old middle school friends still joke with me about it every time I see them.

> # Cut from Basketball Team
>
> - 7th grade
> - cut from tryouts
> - all my friends made it
> - felt horrible
> - 8th grade made team
> - started 1st game!
> - got ball and panicked
> - took a half-court shot
> - benched the rest of the year!
> - friends still laugh about it with me

Now, before you think you are done, quickly write down every theme that you could preach from this story. This is critical for helping you find these stories later. If you are using Evernote, these themes should be your tags.

For example, I would tag my basketball story regret, failure, perseverance, determination, success, embarrassment, middle school, friends, and sports.

4. Get Help (optional)

Here is where this exercise can get surprisingly fun. You don't have to do this alone. In fact, it's better not to.

Have you ever sat around with old friends and told stories? A lot of the time they remember things and bring up stories that you haven't thought about in years. However, as soon as they start talking, all the details come back to you like it happened yesterday.

Use this to your advantage. Get together with a some old friends. Tell them you are gathering stories from your life. Ask them about funny, embarrassing, or life-changing stories they remember from your life together. Write it all down.

Don't just stop with your friends. If you are married, sit down with your wife and stroll down memory lane together. Do the same thing with your parents, sibling, relatives, and co-workers.

If you have kids, they are also a fantastic source. They will remember all kinds of hilarious things that you have said, ridiculous things you have done, messy parenting moments, or crazy things that they did when you weren't paying attention.

Have fun with this, and capture every story that comes up.

5. File Them Away

After doing the work, you better have an organized system for filing these gems.

You can use mine or create your own, but make sure you have a system that allows you to retrieve your illustrations the next time you are preaching about that category.

If you focus, take your time, and do all this, you will walk away with thousands of incredible, real-life stories that will connect with your audience and take your preaching to another level.

Do This

Personal stories will make your preaching more relatable, memorable, authentic, and interesting. The payoff for having hundreds or thousands of these stories at your disposal is enormous.

Warning: this is the point of the book where you nod your head, think to yourself that this is a good idea you should try sometime, then forget about it and never do a thing.

DON'T.

Do this. Do it now. Fire up that brain of yours and wander through the dusty archives of your life. You won't regret it.

You don't have to collect every story in one day. Pace yourself. Set a regular rhythm of working on your illustration database a little bit each day. Before you know it, you will have years worth of great stories.

The stories you capture will be gold. Your preaching will be better for it, and you will save hours every week searching for good illustrations.

CONCLUSION

"How, then, can they call on the one they have not believed in? And how can they believe in the one of whom they have not heard? And how can they hear without someone preaching to them?"
(Romans 10:14, NIV)

One of the pastors I respect most is not flashy. He does not pastor a large church. You will never see his name on the cover of a book or as the speaker at a conference.

But none of that matters. He has been a model of character and integrity in ministry for over 30 years. He is thought well of by his community, respected by his church, and loved by his family.

Over decades, his church has faithfully changed the lives of thousands of people, including mine.

Nearly every Sunday for 30 years he has faithfully preached the Gospel. That is what I call a successful ministry!

I hope we can all strive for such a life in ministry.

The location of your church and size of your audience doesn't change this simple fact: your preaching matters.

You are a steward of the Word of God. The Bible is clear that at the end of our lives, we will all be held accountable for the words we spoke (James 3:1). This is not a calling to be taken lightly.

Grab hold of every opportunity you have to preach. You never know when somebody in the room might be transformed, not by your greatness, but because you were faithful to God's Word and the calling to proclaim it as best you could.

It is my hope that this book has helped you get a better handle on the practical side of preparing a message, and preparing yourself as the messenger.

No matter how difficult the road ahead may get, don't give up!

Every message matters. Every sermon makes a difference.

Even if we don't see the impact immediately, we are planting seeds.

God has given you everything you need to fulfill His calling on your life.

John Wesley once said, "Give me 100 preachers who fear nothing but sin and desire nothing but God; such alone will shake the gates of hell."

May your preaching shake the gates of Hell.

LEARN MORE

If you liked this book and would like to learn more, please visit ProPreacher.com for hundreds of free preaching articles, sermon illustrations, and more.

Also, you can always connect with me on Twitter @ProPreacher or Facebook at facebook.com/propreacher.

Or feel free to shoot me an email at brandon@ProPreacher.com. I would love to hear how the tips in this book have helped you.

ABOUT THE AUTHOR

Hey, I'm Brandon. Thanks for reading my book!

I am the husband to my beautiful wife, Taryn, and father to our two awesome kids.

I have worked as a pastor for in multiple churches across the country from church plants to some of the largest and fastest growing churches in the United States. And I love preaching.

For the last decade I have been on a journey to become the best preacher I can possibly be.

I have preached multiple sermons a week for years. I have worked in different churches absorbing everything I could. I have read every preaching book, blog post and article I can get my hands on. I listened to thousands of sermons. And I'm still learning.

In November of 2012, I started a blog about preaching to write my thoughts from this journey and decided to name it ProPreacher.com. Then I told no one.

I didn't tell anyone because, honestly, I was afraid what people might think. But I also wanted to see if what I wrote would even resonate with people.

I didn't want people to visit my blog because they knew me or I asked them to. I wanted people to come because the content was so compelling and helpful that they wanted to come back for more.

To my surprise, people showed up, came back, and shared it with their friends.

I am blown away by the fact that the ideas and principles I have learned and shared on ProPreacher.com have been read by thousands of pastors around the world.

I don't pretend to be the world's foremost preaching guru. I still have a lot to learn. However, my hope is that the things I have learned and continue to learn will help you as much as they have helped me.

Thanks for taking this ride with me.

– Brandon Hilgemann

Made in the USA
Columbia, SC
17 September 2021